CAMPAIGN 292

CAMDEN 1780

The annihilation of Gates' Grand Army

DAVID SMITH

ILLUSTRATED BY GRAHAM TURNER

Series editor Marcus Cowper

First published in Great Britain in 2016 by Osprey Publishing,
PO Box 883, Oxford, OX1 9PL, UK
PO Box 3985, New York, NY 10185-3985, USA
E-mail: info@ospreypublishing.com

A CIP catalogue record for this book is available from the British Library.

ISBN: 978 1 4728 1285 8
PDF e-book ISBN: 978 1 4728 1286 5
e-Pub ISBN: 978 1 4728 1287 2

Editorial by Ilios Publishing Ltd, Oxford, UK (www.iliospublishing.com)
Index by Alan Rutter
Typeset in Myriad Pro and Sabon
Maps by Bounford.com
3D bird's-eye views by The Black Spot
Battlescene illustrations by Graham Turner
Originated by PDQ Media, Bungay, UK
Printed in China through Worldprint Ltd.

16 17 18 19 20   10 9 8 7 6 5 4 3 2 1

DEDICATION

This book is dedicated to my family – Shirley, Harry and Josh.

ACKNOWLEDGEMENTS

I would like to thank various people for their help in the preparation of this
book: Stuart Morgan for his excellent battlefield photography, David
Reuwer for his expertise and guidance, Werner Willis and Don Troiani for
their magnificent artwork, Chris Mlynarczyk of the 1st Delaware Regiment
organization, Peter Harrington of the Anne S. K. Brown Military Collection,
Mary Jo Fairchild from the Addlestone Library, Joanna Craig from the
Historic Camden Revolutionary War Site, Tracie Logan from the United
States Naval Academy Museum and Marcus Cowper of Ilios Publishing.

ARTIST'S NOTE

Readers may care to note that the original paintings from which the color
plates in this book were prepared are available for private sale. The
Publishers retain all reproduction copyright whatsoever. All enquiries
should be addressed to:

Graham Turner
PO Box 568
Aylesbury
Buckinghamshire
HP17 8ZX
UK
www.studio88.co.uk

The Publishers regret that they can enter into no correspondence upon this
matter.

THE WOODLAND TRUST

Osprey Publishing are supporting the Woodland Trust, the UK's leading
woodland conservation charity, by funding the dedication of trees.

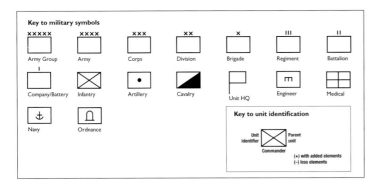

Key to military symbols

Army Group | Army | Corps | Division | Brigade | Regiment | Battalion

Company/Battery | Infantry | Artillery | Cavalry | Unit HQ | Engineer | Medical

Navy | Ordnance

Key to unit identification

Unit identifier | Parent unit
Commander
(+) with added elements
(−) less elements

CONTENTS

British operations in the Southern Theatre, 1776–79

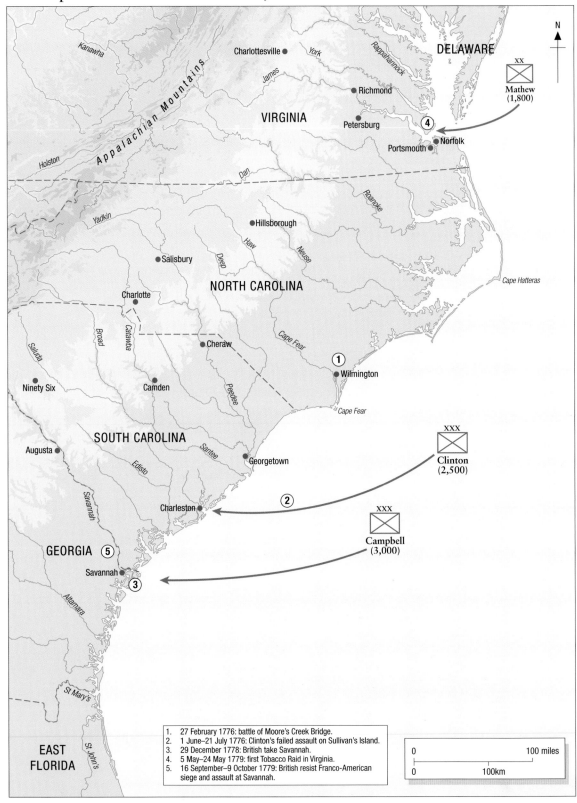

1. 27 February 1776: battle of Moore's Creek Bridge.
2. 1 June–21 July 1776: Clinton's failed assault on Sullivan's Island.
3. 29 December 1778: British take Savannah.
4. 5 May–24 May 1779: first Tobacco Raid in Virginia.
5. 16 September–9 October 1779: British resist Franco-American siege and assault at Savannah.

ORIGINS OF THE CAMPAIGN

The campaign of 1780 had a long gestation period. The surrender of Lieutenant-General John Burgoyne at Saratoga, in October 1777, had fundamentally altered the landscape of the War of Independence, and it was upon this new landscape that British planning now had to operate. The loss of an entire army was a shocking blow and underlined the fact that the previous strategy had not worked.

A period of soul searching followed, as ministers and generals considered a new approach to the war. The major issue at hand was the increasing likelihood that the French would openly enter the war on the side of the colonists. French support had been important from the commencement of hostilities, but the arrival of French ground and (especially) sea forces in North America would drastically change the nature of the war. The American victory at Saratoga was just the sort of thing that might tempt the French to commit themselves openly to the rebel cause.

If, or more likely when, that happened, Britain would find itself painfully stretched. The rebels had proved resilient enough on their own during the first two campaigns of the war, but naval supremacy had remained one of the major cards in Britain's hand. A French fleet in North American waters would be a frightening prospect and could threaten any of the British garrisons scattered through the colonies.

Of even more concern was the potential threat to British possessions in the West Indies. These were far more important, economically, than the North American colonies, and British forces, already spread thinly, would

The loss of a substantial army when John Burgoyne surrendered at Saratoga impacted upon British planning for the rest of the war. (Library of Congress)

need to be relocated to protect Jamaica and a clutch of smaller islands in the Lesser Antilles: Barbuda, Antigua, St Kitts, Nevis, Montserrat, Barbados, St Vincent, Martinique, Guadeloupe and Dominica. Given the near certainty of French intervention in the war, it is remarkable that British planning initially took the hopeful view that it might not happen. Plans were initially made on the assumption that French forces would not arrive to complicate matters.

The first problem the British administration had to face was deciding who would be the commander-in-chief for the 1778 campaign, if the struggle was to be continued. The previous commander, Sir William Howe, had asked for and been granted permission to resign his post, having fallen out with the American Secretary, Lord George Germain.

Surprisingly, the top candidate to command the British army for the 1778 campaign was ... William Howe. This was at least partly because there just did not seem to be any attractive alternative. Howe's second in command, Sir Henry Clinton, was not popular and his prickly manner promised nothing but trouble if he was elevated to overall command. Sir Guy Carleton had been so thoroughly disaffected by his removal from command of the Northern Army for the Saratoga campaign that he was unlikely even to enter into a correspondence with Germain, let alone accept a position from him.

The most energetic general in North America, the sort of man who might actually have waged the kind of campaign Germain had been dreaming of for nearly three years by this point, had just surrendered his army at Saratoga and many other potential candidates were unwilling to serve in America. Serious consideration was therefore given to attempting to persuade Howe to stay on, but eventually it was accepted that he had to go. With some reluctance, on 8 March 1778, Germain wrote to Clinton, informing him that he was to take over as commander-in-chief.

At the same time there was considerable debate over the form the next campaign should take. The opinions of Germain's fellow secretaries of state, Lord Weymouth (Southern) and Lord Suffolk (Northern), were invited. Lord Sandwich at the admiralty and Sir Jeffery Amherst added military insight. This was to be a much more wide-ranging process than that employed for the first two campaigns of the war. There was no pre-ordained strategy to blind everyone to other options, as had been the case with operations along the Hudson in 1776 and 1777, and this was not to be a cosy committee of Germain and his generals. Despite the debate over whether or not to retain Howe as commander, his opinions were not invited, nor was Clinton involved at this stage.

Detailed analyses were submitted by Sandwich and Amherst. Sandwich noted that the need for Lord Howe to use his fleet as a taxi service for his brother's army had tied it up for two campaigns and prevented it from performing what ought to have been its primary function – bottling up rebel shipping and capturing rebel privateers. Sandwich wanted the roles in North America to be flipped; the army should support the navy, by securing more naval bases along the east coast. This would allow a blockade to be effected to strangle the rebels into submission. Sandwich also noted that the war would enter a new phase when the French finally declared open support for the Americans. In that case, Britain would be faced with serious naval opposition, and if Spain joined at the same time, British naval supremacy would be lost. He therefore urged the building of new ships.

When Amherst weighed in with his suggestions, he broadly agreed with Sandwich's assessment. In Amherst's opinion, an effective land-based campaign in North America would require 40,000 reinforcements. Although this figure was probably a realistic assessment, there was no way such extensive reinforcements could be found. Amherst's intention was probably as much intended to show the futility of attempting this kind of war – he, like Sandwich, advocated a naval blockade, in order to force the rebels to accept terms.

Germain took all of the opinions on board in framing his initial orders for Clinton. Those orders underlined the official opinion of Howe's 1777 campaign, which had achieved nothing more than the capture of Philadelphia; Clinton was given permission to evacuate Philadelphia if he decided the troops garrisoning it could be better used elsewhere.

Germain had good news on the subject of reinforcements. Although not approaching Amherst's musings on the need for 40,000 men, they would be, nevertheless, significant. New corps had been authorized by Parliament, while independent gentlemen, as well as cities, had pledged to raise new regiments. The war effort was to be boosted by a new loan of £6,000,000, announced in the budget of March 1778, and Germain reckoned he could deliver 12,000 new British soldiers for Clinton, as well as more German regiments.

Apart from giving Clinton latitude to attempt to bring Washington to a general action, Germain instructed him to cooperate with the navy in a scheme of raids along the coast from New York to Nova Scotia. Germain specified that these raids should be concluded by October 1778, at which point attention should switch to the southern colonies, specifically Georgia and South Carolina.

The beguiling vision of numerous loyalists waiting to take part in the struggle, a recurring theme of British planning, was again conjured up. There was a difference in emphasis this time, however. Rather than looking for loyalists to form or join full-time provincial regiments or companies, they were to act as local forces, holding territory gained by the British and allowing the regular army to move on and pacify new areas. Diversionary raids could be mounted in Virginia and Maryland to prevent the rebels from concentrating forces against the main British effort in Georgia and South Carolina.

In effect, this was a different way of enacting the Hudson Strategy of the first two campaigns of the war. The overall aim was much the same – bringing the northern colonies to their knees by cutting them off from their supply base in the south. While the Hudson Strategy had aimed at physically isolating the northern colonies by dominating the

Despite his lacklustre performance as commander-in-chief (not to mention the fact that he had been given permission to resign) serious consideration was given to retaining William Howe at the head of the British army in America for the 1778 campaign. (Anne S. K. Brown Military Collection, Brown University)

Hudson River, the new strategy aimed to pacify the southern colonies and, in the same way, deny the northern colonies the supplies they needed for their war effort and their very survival.

It was a sensible, manageable strategy, the product of careful reflection, calm reassessment and realistic goals. It reflected a new understanding of the nature of the war and the difficulty in imposing a purely military solution upon the rebels. Clinton was never to get the opportunity to enact it.

FRENCH INTERVENTION

As well as the change in strategy, Britain also contemplated a negotiated settlement. A new peace effort, the Carlisle Commission, offered significant concessions but ultimately achieved nothing. So soon after Saratoga, the Americans were willing to negotiate only on a timetable for British withdrawal from the colonies. Germain appears to have been almost ridiculously confident in the prospects for a negotiated peace, informing Clinton that he could not imagine a campaign would be needed in 1778, so certain was the commission of success.

As unrealistic as Germain's confidence appears, however, the French were also concerned that serious concessions by the British might lead to a patching-up with the colonists. News of the terms the Carlisle Commission was ready to offer seems to have brought forward French plans for a treaty with the rebels. Just days after Germain had written to Clinton outlining the strategy for the next campaign, the French ambassador informed London that such a treaty was now in place.

British planning needed another radical rethink. Clinton's orders were still sitting on a ship waiting to sail to America, but they would soon be joined by another letter. This outlined a very different policy for Clinton to follow; the American war had been relegated to secondary importance. Far from receiving a healthy number of reinforcements, Clinton was now ordered to provide troops for operations elsewhere, including 5,000 men for an expedition against French-held St Lucia. The reduced nature of his army rendered the abandonment of Philadelphia a necessity and Clinton was also given discretion to evacuate New York if he believed that was advisable. The cities that Howe had spent two campaigns in capturing were now considered expendable. Clinton reached Philadelphia, ready to take over from Howe, on 8 May. Both letters from Germain were waiting for him, which was a particularly cruel introduction to the position of commander-in-chief.

Jeffery Amherst (depicted here in medieval armour, which was the style in military portraiture) was one of the key figures consulted over possible plans for the war following the failure of the Hudson Strategy in both 1776 and 1777. (Anne S. K. Brown Military Collection)

The 1778 campaign was therefore one of reorganization. Offensive operations took a back seat as Clinton managed the tricky business of extricating his army from Philadelphia and relocating to New York. It was not until the end of the year that the first concrete step was taken in the implementation of the new strategy. A small army under Lieutenant-Colonel Archibald Campbell captured Savannah, Georgia, for the loss of four killed and five wounded and, for once, dreams of loyalist strength appeared to have been justified. 'Shoals flock to the royal standard daily,' said Campbell, 'and I have got the country in arms against the Congress. I have taken a stripe and a star from the rebel flag of America.'

At the same time, the entry of France into the war had threatened to change the entire nature of the conflict. 'The Americans,' Germain spluttered in the House of Commons, 'by their alliance, are become French, and should in future be treated as Frenchmen.' There were few things more terrifying in the 18th century than being told that the British viewed you as a Frenchman, and it appeared that the war might be entering an altogether darker phase. Britain finally had an enemy it could despise, and, as well as concern over the new forces now ranged against it, there was also relish.

French intervention might have delivered an early knockout blow if a force under the Comte d'Estaing had been able to defeat Lord Howe's British fleet and capture either Clinton's army on its retreat from Philadelphia, or the garrison at Rhode Island. D'Estaing was to have a further opportunity to wreak havoc when he sailed south to the West Indies in November of 1778. Unknown to him, the 5,000 men ordered to St Lucia were sailing on a parallel course. The soldiers, experienced British troops that Clinton agonized over losing, reached St Lucia safely, but were never able to return to Clinton. With a reduced army, Clinton submitted one of his regular requests to be given permission to resign his post. It was refused (the ministry was running out of generals) and he descended into a near-paranoid state of mind early in 1779. The result was that the southern strategy was effectively shelved for a full year after the fall of Savannah.

There was also the small matter of replacing Admiral Howe, who had resigned his position as naval commander-in-chief in support of his brother, the general. Clinton was well aware of the need for army and naval forces to cooperate harmoniously – he had been a begrudging admirer of the efficiency with which the Howe brothers had worked together. He also rated himself very highly as an expert on naval matters and took the liberty of submitting a shortlist of suitable candidates for the job. His shortlist was ignored and the post was awarded to Mariot Arbuthnot. It is difficult to imagine a more unsuitable working partner for Clinton, and their tortured relationship was to have a profoundly negative impact on the British war effort.

While awaiting the arrival of Arbuthnot (who did not reach New York until the summer of 1779), Clinton initiated a plan to engage the main rebel army under George Washington. Defeating the rebel army had never been officially dropped as a war aim, although it had been relegated in importance, and Clinton still saw it as an essential element of the new southern strategy. Only by removing Washington as a threat would he be free to detach sufficient forces for a southern offensive. Clinton hoped that by taking American-held positions in the Hudson Highlands, at Stony Point and Verplancks, he could force the rebel general into a full-scale action, but Washington refused to be drawn and Clinton was forced to abandon his scheme and turn his thoughts southwards.

There was some reason for optimism. Clinton's latest attempt to resign had at least convinced Germain of the need to offer reinforcements for the disgruntled general. More than 6,000 men were apparently on their way with Arbuthnot, theoretically giving Clinton enough men to resurrect the southern strategy almost two years after it had first been adopted. There was room for pessimism as well. The Spanish, eager to win back Gibraltar and possibly capture Jamaica, signed an offensive alliance with France in June. British forces now had even more territory to protect.

Clinton remained morose. To a confidante he claimed, 'Let me advise you never to take command of an army. I know I am hated – nay, detested – in this army. I am determined to return home; the Minister has used me so ill that I can no longer bear with this life.'

When Arbuthnot arrived, Clinton was appalled at the frail appearance of the admiral. He was equally appalled at finding only 4,000 reinforcements on the newly arrived ships, many of whom were ill from a long crossing. An element of farce entered proceedings as the reinforcements were allowed to disembark and spread their infections among the healthy troops. Soon, 6,000 men of Clinton's army were sick.

In what was rapidly becoming a procession of disappointments, news arrived that d'Estaing was on the move again, apparently threatening Jamaica. Clinton again had to detach men to the West Indies, sending Lord Cornwallis with 4,000 troops to defend the island. The offensive in the south was on the back burner once more, but matters changed dramatically when it was learned that d'Estaing had actually arrived off the coast of Savannah. The one British foothold in the south, which also had the potential to act as a vital link between North American and West Indies possessions, was threatened.

Clinton was forced to confront the painful necessity of abandoning the British base at Newport, Rhode Island. Captured by Clinton himself at the end of the 1776 campaign, it tied up 5,000 men in garrison duty and was too ripe a plum to leave dangling for d'Estaing. Newport was evacuated, and although this is now generally reckoned to have been a mistake, at the time Germain responded with approval, on the assumption that the extra troops and ships would allow for operations in the south. Fortunately for the British, d'Estaing botched his siege of Savannah badly. Despite enjoying complete command of the sea and outnumbering the British by around 5,000 to 3,000, he opted for a rash assault on 9 October that was repulsed with heavy losses. D'Estaing had failed again, but Britain was using up its store of luck at a frightening rate.

At the end of 1779, despite his precarious position, with naval supremacy ever liable to shift with the arrival and departure of enemy fleets, Clinton turned his thoughts once more to the southern theatre. He pondered the options available to him, considering three scenarios. The first was continuing British superiority on land and at sea, which would allow him to pursue a decisive battle with Washington or shift attention to the southern colonies. The second scenario was superiority only on land, which would necessitate a concentration of force to avoid being defeated in detachments. Finally, superiority at sea but not on land would impose a naval-only strategy of coastal raids and blockade.

The dashing Polish cavalry commander Casimir Pulaski died during the wasteful assault on British-held Savannah at the end of 1779. (Anne S. K. Brown Military Collection)

There was nothing particularly insightful about Clinton's assessment, yet he proceeded to disregard it completely. Britain had already lost naval supremacy on several occasions and it had almost spelled disaster at New York, Rhode Island and Savannah. Indeed, Newport had been evacuated for the very reason that naval supremacy could not be guaranteed. This would seem to fit squarely into Clinton's second scenario, enforcing a concentration of force rather than a dispersal. Despite this, Clinton now planned to shift a substantial army to the south to take Charleston and effect the pacification of South Carolina. It was a roll of the dice, and the final verdict on Clinton's decision must take into account the fact that the path he chose in December 1779 ultimately led to Yorktown in October 1781.

CHRONOLOGY

1776

27 February	Loyalists defeated at Moore's Creek Bridge.
1 June to 21 July	Failed operation against Sullivan's Island, Charleston.

1777

17 October	Burgoyne surrenders his army at Saratoga.

1778

29 December	British capture Savannah, Georgia.

1779

| 16 September to 9 October | British resist Franco-American siege and assault at Savannah. |
| 26 December | British army sails from New York, bound for Charleston. |

SIEGE OF CHARLESTON, 1780

14 February	British army lands at Simmons Island.
19 March	Clinton learns he will not be allowed to resign his position.
20 March	Arbuthnot gets frigates over the bar.
1 April	Siegeworks opened.
7 April	First British parallel is completed.
7 April	Virginia Continentals reinforce Charleston.
8 April	Arbuthnot's ships pass Fort Moultrie on Sullivan's Island.
10 April	Clinton offers terms to Charleston garrison.
12 April	Webster sent to secure upper Cooper with 1,500 men.
14 April	Fire breaks out in Charleston from artillery bombardment.
14 April	Tarleton launches night attack at Monck's Corner.
17 April	Second parallel completed.
18 April	British reinforcements arrive from New York.
23–24 April	Americans launch sally against third parallel.
1 May	Defensive canal breached.
6 May	Tarleton destroys American force at Lenud's Ferry.
6 May	Third parallel completed.
7 May	British capture Fort Moultrie.
9–10 May	Bombardment of Charleston.
10 May	News arrives of approach of French fleet.
11 May	Lincoln accepts Clinton's terms.

CAMDEN CAMPAIGN, 1780

16 April	Reinforcements under de Kalb head south from Morristown.
18 May	Cornwallis leaves Charleston for Camden.
26 May	Nisbet Balfour and Patrick Ferguson set out for Ninety Six.
29 May	Tarleton catches Buford at Waxhaws ('Buford's Massacre').
3 June	Clinton issues the third and most damaging of his proclamations.
8 June	Clinton sets sail for New York.
20 June	Loyalists scattered at Ramsour's Mill.
21 June	Cornwallis returns to Charleston.
12 July	Loyalists defeated at Williamson's Plantation ('Huck's Defeat').
24 July	Gates takes command of the American army.
30 July	Sumter attacks British post at Rocky Mount (repulsed).
6 August	Sumter attacks British post near Hanging Rock (repulsed).
7 August	Gates joins 1,200 North Carolina militia under Caswell.
13 August	Gates takes position at Rugeley's Mills.
14 August	Gates is joined by 700 Virginia militia under Stevens.
15–16 August	Night march of both British and American armies.
16 August	The battle of Camden.
18 August	Tarleton scatters Sumter's force at Fishing Creek.

1780

7 October	Ferguson killed at battle of King's Mountain.

1781

17 January	Tarleton defeated at battle of Cowpens.
15 March	Cornwallis earns costly victory at battle of Guilford Courthouse.
25 April	Battle of Hobkirk's Hill (Second Battle of Camden).
12 May	Cornwallis moves into Virginia.
19 October	Cornwallis surrenders at Yorktown.

OPPOSING COMMANDERS

BRITISH

Lieutenant-General Sir Henry Clinton (1730–95)

Irascible to the point of caricature, Clinton was an enigma to colleagues, friends and family. He appears to have been pathologically incapable of serving harmoniously with either general or admiral and his reputation is not helped by the tiresome thread of self-pity that runs through his correspondence and private notes. His early career included service in the Foot Guards during the Seven Years War (he was an aide-de-camp to Ferdinand of Brunswick) and he was promoted to the rank of major-general by 1772. He sailed to America, along with Howe and Burgoyne, in 1775, although he had lived for several years in the colonies as a youth, when his father served as Governor of New York. The tragedy of Clinton, and what prevents him from merely playing the part of pantomime villain or comic relief, is that his thinking on the war was the most realistic of the many British commanders who tried and failed to solve the riddle of pacifying the colonies. His advice to superiors was bluntly offered, making it unpalatable, but it was usually sound, and he had a far firmer grasp of the strategic realities of the war than the commander-in-chief for the first two campaigns, Sir William Howe. Clinton's great failure was an inability to win others over to his opinion. Had his relationships with Howe, Admiral Mariot Arbuthnot and Lord Cornwallis been better, the outcome of the war might have been very different. Clinton will always deserve credit for being alone in suspecting that Burgoyne's army would run into difficulties on its march from Canada, but again he was unable to convince Howe, and the 1777 campaign was a largely wasted one for Clinton as he sat and fumed in his 'damned starved defensive' at New York while Howe and Burgoyne chased what proved to be an elusive glory elsewhere. Already thoroughly disenchanted with the war, and having threatened repeatedly to resign, he was persuaded to take over as commander-in-chief for the 1778 campaign. Despite serious misgivings and perpetual self-pity over his lack of resources,

Henry Clinton's failure to get on with almost anybody was a problem when he was a subordinate officer, but it had even more serious implications when he was elevated to overall command. (Anne S. K. Brown Military Collection)

this command was to bring him his finest hour, the most complete British victory of the entire war, at Charleston in 1780. From then, however, he was dragged back into stultification at New York while Cornwallis was left to continue the employment of the southern strategy. Following the defeat at Yorktown, Clinton spent much of the remainder of his life trying in vain to clear his name, compiling a detailed account of the war (later published as *The American Rebellion*), which was no doubt aided by the mountain of notes, memos and letters he had hoarded compulsively over the years. His account was not published during his lifetime.

Lieutenant-General Charles, Earl Cornwallis (1738–1805)

Cornwallis was that rare exception among the ranks of British commanders – a general whose reputation survived the American War of Independence. While Howe, Burgoyne and Clinton all sank into obscurity following their efforts in North America, Cornwallis shrugged off the defeat at Yorktown to resurrect his career in India. Cornwallis endeared himself to the American Secretary, Germain, at the very outset of the war, volunteering to serve in a subordinate capacity in the Cape Fear expedition that was planning to leave English shores in November 1775. Cornwallis was a serious soldier, who earned the respect, even love, of his men by sharing their hardships. His regiment, the 33rd, was acknowledged as one of the finest in the British army and when he was given permission to sail to North America, his regiment went with him. As a major-general in 1775, Cornwallis served underneath Henry Clinton, but their working relationship got off to an uncertain start with the fiasco of the assault on the rebel fort on Sullivan's Island, guarding the approach to Charleston harbour. It was just the first of several events that served to drive a wedge gradually between the two men; yet even as late as 1779, Cornwallis was open to a rapprochement. Devastated by the death of his beloved wife, Cornwallis assured Clinton that coming back out to America would be a blessing for him. 'If you should think that you can have any material employment for me,' he wrote to Clinton in April, 'send for me and I will most readily come to you. I really shall come with pleasure.' Cornwallis might have been happy enough to serve with Clinton once more, but it was the army and active duty that he really craved. Their relationship soured during the siege of Charleston and by the time Clinton headed back to New York, leaving Cornwallis in command in the south, the two were effectively estranged. Cornwallis survived the disgrace of Yorktown largely because he was able to frame the story of the debacle, casting Clinton as the guilty party.

A naturally aggressive commander, Cornwallis was uncomfortable as a subordinate to Clinton and relished the chance to operate independently when his commander-in-chief headed back to New York after the fall of Charleston. (Anne S. K. Brown Military Collection)

If Cornwallis was aggressive, a new word would need to be invented for Banastre Tarleton. He pushed the men (and horses) under his command relentlessly and the only people he showed less mercy to were his enemies. (Anne S. K. Brown Military Collection)

Lieutenant-Colonel Banastre Tarleton (1754–1833)

There are few more polarizing figures in the story of the War of Independence than the commander of the British Legion. Vilified by the patriots, lionized by the British, he was one of the most uncompromising soldiers in the war and pursued his goals with a single-mindedness that was rare on the British side. Tarleton made his mark quickly after reaching the colonies in the middle of 1776. As a cornet in the light dragoons he helped capture the rebel general, Charles Lee, towards the end of the campaign. In 1778 he was placed in command of the combined provincial force known as the British Legion and it was at the head of these men that his ruthless reputation was cemented. Known as 'Bloody Ban' by the patriots, he evoked fear and hatred in equal measure among his enemies. He came badly unstuck when his impetuous approach to battlefield tactics backfired against Daniel Morgan at Cowpens, but during the Camden campaign he was nothing short of a holy terror.

Admiral Mariot Arbuthnot (1711–94)

The fact that few people, whether contemporaries or historians, have had a good word to say about Mariot Arbuthnot makes it remarkable that he was chosen to succeed Lord Howe as commander-in-chief of British naval forces in North America. A captain up until 1775, he was named naval commissioner at Halifax in that year and promoted to rear-admiral in 1778, already in his mid-60s. His appointment to the overall command in North America in 1779 has been characterized as a monumental blunder by Lord Sandwich, but also as a deliberate snub to Clinton, who had suggested several other suitable candidates for the position. Arbuthnot's lack of cooperation with Clinton during the siege of Charleston fatally undermined a relationship that had never had much chance of success and their ensuing inability to work together against a French fleet at Rhode Island was sadly predictable. It is always dangerous to rely on long-accepted opinions about officers and in Arbuthnot's

Old and shaky by the time he was surprisingly named as Britain's naval commander-in-chief in America, Mariot Arbuthnot showed an unwillingness to cooperate with Clinton that fatally doomed their relationship. (Anne S. K. Brown Military Collection)

case there appears to be some evidence that he was actually unwell during his time at the head of the British fleet, some historians having suggested he had suffered a series of strokes that impacted on his mental and physical abilities. Certainly he was an ineffective commander, William B. Willcox commenting, 'His tactics were uninspired, if dogged, and his strategic ideas often ludicrous.' After falling out with Admiral George Rodney over the latter's assumption of command for a short spell in 1780 (Rodney was the superior officer and Arbuthnot displayed a curious bullheadedness in refusing to accept this simple and inescapable fact), Arbuthnot joined the long list of British commanders-in-chief from both services to ask leave to resign their posts. He was succeeded by Admiral Thomas Graves in 1781. A particularly cruel biography states that Arbuthnot became clinically dead in 1794, but that professionally he had already been dead for years.

AMERICAN

Benjamin Lincoln (1733–1810)

It was easy to underestimate Lincoln, a rotund figure with sagging cheeks, as a military man, but he earned his post as commander of the Southern Department, having caught the eye of George Washington in operations in the northern theatre. A farmer and militia officer from Massachusetts, he was a lieutenant-colonel of militia in 1772 and had risen to major-general by May 1776. He commanded a wing of Washington's army at the battle of White Plains and it was on Washington's recommendation that Lincoln was promoted to major-general in the Continental Army in February 1777,

Benjamin Lincoln faced an almost impossible challenge at Charleston. He recognized the potential benefits of extricating his army before it was too late, but was under intense pressure not to abandon the city. (Print Collection, Miriam and Ira D. Wallach Division of Arts, Prints and Photographs, The New York Public Library)

inadvertently invoking the ire of Benedict Arnold, who was overlooked. 'An active, spirited, sensible man,' in the words of Washington, Lincoln served with distinction. He was badly wounded in the right ankle during the Saratoga campaign (leaving him with a permanent limp, as the healed leg was left two inches shorter) but after a lengthy recuperation he was given command of the Southern Department. Lincoln appears to have been shaken by events in South Carolina and Georgia in 1779. Following the capture of Savannah by the British, Lincoln arrived to counter the move. Threatening Augusta, he was surprised by a bold strike by the British commander, Archibald Campbell, against Charleston. Lincoln was forced to hurry back to save the city and became reluctant to leave it again, which impacted on its defence in 1780. Following the fall of Charleston, Lincoln was exchanged for two generals and took part in the Yorktown campaign. He became Secretary of War in October 1781. A deep-thinking man, he wrote several scientific papers and was also awarded an MA from Harvard.

Controversy still surrounds Horatio Gates' actions following the battle of Camden. Limited in his capacities as a battlefield general, he excelled as an organizer and administrator. (Anne S. K. Brown Military Collection)

Horatio Gates (1727–1806)

Gates is remembered equally as the hero of Saratoga and the architect of disaster at Camden, but it is probably true that neither reputation is fully deserved. He eked out a career in the British army, seeing experience in the French and Indian War (he was badly wounded in the battle of Monongahela), but he eventually hit the glass ceiling because of a lack of influential patrons. When the British army was returned to its peacetime establishment following the war, Gates was placed on half pay and his career appeared to be over. Somewhat embittered, he started a new life in Virginia and was a natural candidate for a position in the fledgling American army in 1775, serving first as George Washington's adjutant general. Where Gates really stood out was in the field of army organization and administration, in which area he worked wonders, but he also had his own ideas on strategy and these were cautious; he favoured waiting the British out, allowing the burden of expense to sap their appetite for the war. Credit for the victory at Saratoga naturally fell on Gates, who was in command of American forces at the time, but Philip Schuyler deserved a share. (It is possible that Gates developed too strong a regard for militia following his experiences on the Saratoga campaign and he certainly seems to have had too much confidence in them at Camden.) Gates wanted to follow up Saratoga with an invasion of Canada and this put him at loggerheads with Washington – for a time it appeared that Gates might replace the commander-in-chief and their relationship never fully recovered. Washington was not in favour of Gates taking command in the Southern Department in 1780 and his misgivings were borne out by the disastrous Camden campaign, although no official charges were brought against Gates (he repeatedly demanded a court martial in order to clear his name), and he was reinstated in the army in 1782. After the war, Gates famously freed his slaves before moving to New York, where he spent a good deal of his second wife's vast personal fortune in aiding army veterans.

Johann 'Baron' de Kalb (1721–80)

Born to a humble family on 19 June 1721, Johann Kalb later claimed the title of 'Baron', to which he was not entitled, to enable him to progress in the army. It was a pragmatic decision, 'best calculated to lift him out of the narrow confines of his native condition into a more advantageous position' in the words of his biographer, Friedrich Kapp. Following service in the French army (without a title this would have been impossible), de Kalb's military career appeared to be at an end by 1777, when he was offered a place in the American army as one of the group of European advisers who added a dash of veteran savvy to the desperately inexperienced American military. He had to wait a long time for his first taste of action, which followed his appointment as commander of a force of Continentals sent southwards to aid in the defence of Charleston. De Kalb was to perform with great bravery in the doomed struggle at Camden.

Commodore Abraham Whipple (1733–1819)

Whipple burst onto the scene as tensions rose in the colonies, heading the band that burned the British revenue cutter, *Gaspee*, in 1772. This set the tone for a swashbuckling career in which he became a captain in the Continental Navy in 1775, seized military supplies from a British base in the Bahamas and captured numerous prizes. His most lucrative action took place in July 1779, when he took 11 British vessels on the same day with a combined prize value of more than a million dollars. Following this he was placed in command of American naval forces at Charleston, where his conduct became decidedly more cautious. Three US Navy ships have been named in his honour.

De Kalb was appalled by the lack of support offered to his small army as it made its way southwards to reinforce Charleston and was relieved to hand over command to Gates. (Anne S. K. Brown Military Collection)

OPPOSING ARMIES

BRITISH FORCES

The fighting in the American south in 1780 and 1781 was chiefly undertaken by small armies and even smaller bands of men with varying levels of organization. The War of Independence was always fought on a relatively small scale by 18th-century standards, but even the 20,000-strong armies of the early campaigns were a distant memory as Clinton moved south in an attempt to change the course of the war as well as the location.

The veterans of Cornwallis's own regiment had been tempered by multiple campaigns in North America and were considered to be among the elite of the British army. They would suffer badly at Camden. (Painting by Don Troiani)

After five years of fighting, both sides could call on hardened, experienced troops, although both sides were also finding such men to be in short supply. Clinton had delayed his move southwards for the simple reason that he did not have enough men to hold New York and embark on a major offensive at the same time. Reinforcements from England (though fewer in number than he had been led to expect), as well as the freeing up of the garrison at Rhode Island, had helped. The dispatch of 5,000 British regulars to St Lucia in 1778 had not. It was a small army that Clinton embarked at New York in December 1779, but it was an experienced one.

British regulars formed the heart of the army, but their regiments had been steadily whittled down over years of active service. Leading the way would be the men of the combined light infantry battalions, composed of the light companies of the various British regiments. Numbering nearly 1,300 men and split into two battalions, these were the best troops in the British army and had benefited from two campaigns under the directorship of the former commander-in-chief Sir William Howe, a light infantry expert. Two composite grenadier battalions were also something of an elite unit, offering around 1,100 men between them.

The 33rd Regiment, Cornwallis's own, had long been considered one of the best regiments in the British army. By the end of 1779 its numbers had been reduced to just 463 and, by the battle of Camden on 16 August 1780, it had dwindled still further to less than 300. Active duty was not the only problem – the climate in the southern colonies took its toll, especially on unseasoned troops, with fevers and heat exhaustion picking off many men. The 71st Regiment, a two-battalion unit, could muster over 850 men and five more regiments, the 7th, 23rd, 60th, 63rd and 64th comprised the rest of Clinton's British regulars.

Cavalry forces had proved to be an Achilles heel for the British throughout the war. In the northern theatre this had not been too much of an impediment (the terrain was unsuited to cavalry actions) but in the south they were essential. The 17th Light Dragoons brought 73 men south and Banastre Tarleton's British Legion included more than 200 mounted troops. The problem here was that most of the army's horses would be lost during the voyage south and it would take time for them to be replaced. When operating at full strength, however, Tarleton in particular would demonstrate the value of a fast-moving force that could pursue, catch and destroy enemy units.

Clinton would also call for reinforcements from New York, bringing the renowned 42nd Regiment (a welcome addition of almost 800 men) as well as experienced provincial units including the Prince of Wales American Regiment, the Queen's Rangers, and the Volunteers of Ireland. The last of these units was to play a prominent part in the battle of Camden and its young commanding officer, Colonel Francis Lord Rawdon, was to serve with great distinction.

Hessian units, the divisive hired help that had bulked up Howe's army through the first two campaigns of the war, were not destined for a major role in the south, but a familiar face did accompany Clinton. Captain Johann Ewald made the voyage along with more than 200 of the elite Hessian Jägers. Howe had come to view these as the finest soldiers in his army, even valuing them more highly than his beloved British light infantry, and Clinton appears to have had an equally high opinion of them judging by his use of them in the siege of Charleston. More than 1,500 Hessian grenadiers also travelled to Charleston and the Regiment von Ditfurth was among the reinforcements summoned from New York. At the opening of the campaign Britain made little use of loyalist militia, but this changed as the campaign progressed and more loyalists declared their willingness to serve. A smattering of South Carolina and Georgia loyalists took part in the siege of Charleston.

Clinton relied heavily on the naval forces of Admiral Mariot Arbuthnot, which included two 74s and two 64s. The arrival of a substantial French fleet could at any moment throw British plans into disorder, but in the absence of such a threat Arbuthnot ought theoretically to have been able to offer Clinton support in moving and supplying his troops and in completing the investiture of Charleston. In reality, such cooperation never materialized. Clinton did, however, get support from Arbuthnot when it came to rebuilding his siege train after the voyage to Charleston. Arbuthnot delivered many of his ships' guns to Clinton after the bulk of the army's artillery had been lost during a tempestuous voyage and more guns were brought in from the Bahamas and St Augustine.

Provincial units like the Volunteers of Ireland, commanded by Lord Rawdon, had become essential and dependable components of the British army by the time the war moved southwards. (Painting by Don Troiani)

Although many Continental Army soldiers were regulars in name only at the start of the war, by 1780 they had been moulded into highly respectable, experienced troops. Regiments from Maryland and Delaware were a match for the British regiments ranged against them. (Anne S. K. Brown Military Collection)

AMERICAN FORCES

The Americans could also by now call upon experienced soldiers in the form of the battle-hardened Continental regiments, but they also made more use of temporary militia forces. This had paid dividends at Saratoga and would again at King's Mountain and other engagements, but at Charleston and Camden the militia accomplished little of worth. It was the Continentals of South Carolina, North Carolina and Virginia that Benjamin Lincoln would rely upon in the siege of Charleston and it would be the Marylanders and Delaware regiments that would bear the brunt of the fighting at Camden.

The Americans were blessed with some formidable fighting men, notably Brigadier-General William Moultrie of the South Carolina Continental Brigade and Lieutenant-Colonel John Laurens of the small composite light infantry unit of just 175 men. The arrival of the 1st Virginia Brigade, on 8 April, brought nearly 900 men within the Charleston defences, but this ultimately served only to increase the haul of prisoners the British took on the surrender of the city. The veteran Continentals were thrown away in the defence of Charleston, with hundreds dying in captivity on prison ships and hundreds more taking the only apparent alternative – service with the British in the West Indies. With little actual fighting during the siege, the various militia units had little to do other than consume supplies, which was not problematic as long as a supply route into the city over the Cooper River was kept open.

American naval forces could not hope to match the big guns of the British ships of the line, but they had an ace up their sleeve, the treacherous bar that guarded access to Charleston harbour. Too shallow for major warships to pass, the result was that only British frigates would be able to engage the ships of Commodore Whipple. A naval confrontation would have been interesting, but never took place.

After the fall of Charleston it was a different American army that contested the field at Camden. Many of the militia were freed on parole and following Clinton's proclamation of 3 June many of these no doubt rejoined the fight against the British. However, almost all of the militia under Gates at Camden were from North Carolina and Virginia, helping to explain their wretched performance. The South Carolina militia nevertheless played their part, and a hugely important part at that, in contesting British control of the colony as they spread forces into the back-country following the fall of Charleston. The heart of Gates' army were the two Maryland brigades, comprising veterans from Maryland and Delaware. Around 900 of these men stood firm at Camden and Gates could have counted on even more had he not detached 100 Marylanders to fight with Sumter.

A vast amount of artillery was lost at Charleston and Gates had to make do with a small artillery force at Camden of just seven or eight guns. He was also deficient in cavalry, having declared that the terrain was not suited to mounted troops.

Historians have to resist the temptation to play 'what if', but it is impossible not to wonder what might have happened in South Carolina had Lincoln followed his urge to extricate his precious Continental units from Charleston while he had the chance. The British had a difficult enough time of it as it was, but the hundreds of Continental troops that ended their war on prison ships or in the West Indies would no doubt have made more of an impact on the battlefield.

ORDERS OF BATTLE

SIEGE OF CHARLESTON

BRITISH FORCES

Lieutenant	General Sir Henry Clinton
Light Infantry	Major-General Alexander Leslie
1st Battalion	Lieutenant-Colonel Robert Abercromby (640)

7th, 22nd, 33rd, 37th, 42nd, 54th, 63rd, 70th, 74th regiments light infantry companies.

Amusettes 4

2nd Battalion	Lieutenant-Colonel Thomas Dundas (637)

23rd, 38th, 43rd, 57th, 64th, 76th, 80th regiments light infantry companies.

84th Regiment 2nd Battalion light infantry company.

Grenadiers

1st Battalion	Lieutenant-Colonel Henry Hope (611)

7th, 17th, 23rd, 33rd, 37th, 38th, 42nd, 43rd regiments grenadier companies.

2nd Battalion	Lieutenant-Colonel John Yorke (526)

22nd, 54th, 57th, 63rd, 64th, 70th, 74th regiments grenadier companies.

7th Regiment	Lieutenant-Colonel Alured Clarke (463)
23rd Regiment	Lieutenant-Colonel Nisbet Balfour (400)
33rd Regiment	Major William Dansey (450)
60th Regiment (2nd Battalion)	Captain Benjamin Wickham (45)
63rd Regiment	Major James Wemyss (400)
64th Regiment	Major Robert McLeroth (350)
Royal Regiment of Artillery	Major Peter Traille (200)
Royal Navy Artillery	Captain George Keith Elphinstone
Corps of Guides and Pioneers	Colonel Beverly Robinson (72)
Brigade of Engineers	Major James Moncrief
Black Pioneers Provincial Unit	Captain Allan Stewart

HESSIAN UNITS

Hesse-Kassel Feld Jäger Korps	Lieutenant-Colonel Ludwig Johann Adolph von Wurmb (224)
Hessian Grenadiers	
1st Battalion	Lieutenant-Colonel Otto Wilhelm von Linsingen (350)
2nd Battalion	Lieutenant-Colonel von Lengercke (360)
3rd Battalion	Lieutenant-Colonel Friedrich von Schuter (365)
4th Battalion	Major Wilhelm Graff (450)
Hesse-Kassel Garrison Regiment von Benning	Colonel Friedrich von Benning
Hesse-Kassel Garrison Regiment von Wissenbach	Lieutenant-Colonel Fredrich von Porbeck

PROVINCIAL UNITS

King's American Regiment	Colonel Edmund Fanning (100)

REINFORCEMENTS FROM GEORGIA

Brigadier-General James Paterson

71st Regiment	Lieutenant-Colonel Alexander McDonald
1st Battalion (378)	
2nd Battalion (491)	

Light Infantry (243)

16th, 71st, New Jersey Volunteers (3rd Battalion) light companies

17th Regiment of Light Dragoons	Captain William Henry Talbot (73)
Brigade of Engineers	Captain Angus Campbell

Black Pioneers (206)

British Legion	Lieutenant-Colonel Banastre Tarleton

Legion Infantry Major Charles Cochrane (287)

Legion Cavalry Lieutenant-Colonel Banastre Tarleton (211)

American Volunteers Major Patrick Ferguson (335)

South Carolina Royalists Colonel Alexander Innes

1st Battalion Lieutenant-Colonel Joseph Robinson (c.90)

2nd Battalion Lieutenant-Colonel Evan McLauren (115)

Royal North Carolina Regiment Lieutenant-Colonel John Hamilton

Georgia Loyalists Major James Wright (32)

Georgia Dragoons Captain Archibald Campbell (40)

New York Volunteers Lieutenant-Colonel George Turnbull

REINFORCEMENTS FROM NEW YORK

Colonel Max von Westerhagen

42nd Regiment Lieutenant-Colonel Duncan McPherson (783)

Hesse-Kassel Fusilier Regiment von Ditfurth Colonel Max von Westerhagen

Prince of Wales American Regiment Lieutenant-Colonel Thomas Pattinson (334)

Queen's Rangers Lieutenant-Colonel John Graves Simcoe (200)

Volunteers of Ireland Colonel Francis Lord Rawdon (423)

King's Orange Rangers

ROYAL NAVY FORCES

Admiral Mariot Arbuthnot

Russell 74 (guns)

Robust 74

Europe 64

Raisonable 64

Renown 50

Romulus 44

Roebuck 44

Blonde 32

Perseus 32

Redmond 32

Raleigh 28

Virginia 28

Camilla 20

Armed Transports 5

Armed Schooners 3

Armed Galleys 2

Row Galleys 3

AMERICAN FORCES

Major-General Benjamin Lincoln

South Carolina Continental Brigade Brigadier-General William Moultrie

1st South Carolina Regiment Colonel Charles Cotesworth Pinckney (231)

2nd South Carolina Regiment Lieutenant-Colonel Francis Marion (266)

3rd South Carolina (Ranger) Regiment Lieutenant-Colonel

William Henderson (302)

North Carolina Continental Brigade Brigadier-General James Hogun

1st North Carolina Regiment Colonel Thomas Clark (260)

2nd North Carolina Regiment Colonel John Patten (244)

3rd North Carolina Regiment Lieutenant Colonel-Commandant Robert Mebane (94)

Light Infantry Corps Lieutenant-Colonel John Laurens (175)

2nd Virginia Brigade Colonel Richard Parker

1st Virginia Detachment Lieutenant-Colonel Samuel Hopkins (258)

2nd Virginia Detachment Colonel William Heth (323)

Hick's South Carolina Militia Regiment (23)

Battalion of North Carolina Volunteers Lieutenant-Colonel Archibald Lytle (202)

1st and 3rd Continental Light Dragoons Captain Robert Yancey (31)

Georgia Regiment of Horse Rangers Colonel Leonard Marbury (41)

Georgia Continental Officers Colonel John White (6)

North Carolina Dragoons Colonel Marquis Francis de Malmedy (41)

Brigade of Artillery Colonel Bernard Beeckman (391 guns)

American Engineer Corps Brigadier-General Louis le Bégue de Presle Duportail

Slaves (600)

Brigade of Militia Brigadier-General Alexander Lillington

Brigade of South Carolina Militia Brigadier-General Lachlan McIntosh (300 estimated)

Brigade of North Carolina Militia Brigadier-General Henry William Harrington (1,700 estimated)

Virginia Militia

Charleston Militia Brigade Colonel Maurice Simons (787)

Volunteer Corps (non-English speaking foreigners) Colonel Marquis de Britigney (125)

AMERICAN REINFORCEMENTS

Brigadier-General William Woodford

1st Virginia Brigade (arrived in Charleston on 8 April) Brigadier-General William Woodford

1st Virginia Regiment Colonel William Russell (336)

2nd Virginia Regiment Colonel John Neville (306)

3rd Virginia Regiment Colonel Nathaniel Gist (252)

AMERICAN NAVAL FORCES

Commodore Abraham Whipple

Boston 46 (guns)

Bricole 44

Zephyr 36

Providence 32

Queen of France 28

L'Aventure 26
Truite 26
General Moultrie 20
Ranger 20
Notre Dame 16
Armed Galleys 3

BATTLE OF CAMDEN, 16 AUGUST 1780

BRITISH FORCES

Lieutenant-General Charles, Lord Cornwallis

(Numbers quoted are officers/men from the 15 August returns.)

Webster's Brigade	Lieutenant-Colonel James Webster
23rd Regiment	Lieutenant-Colonel Nesbit Balfour (10/282)
33rd Regiment	Major William Dansey (14/284)
Light Companies	Captain Charles Campbell (7/141)
Rawdon's Brigade	Colonel Francis Lord Rawdon
Volunteers of Ireland	Colonel Francis Lord Rawdon (15/288)
Royal North Carolina Regiment	Lieutenant-Colonel John Hamilton (20/247)
North Carolina Volunteers (14/188)	
Reserve	Lieutenant-Colonel Alexander McDonald
1st Battalion, 71st Regiment	Captain Hugh Campbell (19/135)
2nd Battalion, 71st Regiment (7/103)	
British Legion	Lieutenant-Colonel Banastre Tarleton
British Legion Cavalry	Major George Hanger (11/171)
British Legion Infantry	Captain Patrick Stewart (8/118)
Royal Regiment of Artillery (2/17)	
3rd Battalion	Lieutenant John MacLeod
Number 1 Company	
6-pdrs (2)	
3-pdrs (2)	
4th Battalion	Lieutenant William Marquois
Number 6 Company	
6-pdrs (2)	
Additional artillery (manned by men from other regiments)	
2-pdrs (2)	
Swivel guns (3)	
Artillery manned by the British Legion	
3-pdrs (1)	
Corps of Guides and Pioneers	Lieutenant Andrew Husband (2/26)

Total 129/220

AMERICAN FORCES

Major-General Horatio Gates

(Strengths are estimated)

First Maryland Brigade	Major-General William Smallwood (400)
1st Maryland Regiment	Lieutenant-Colonel Peter Adams
3rd Maryland Regiment	Major Archibald Anderson
5th Maryland Regiment	Colonel William Richardson
7th Maryland Regiment	Colonel John Gunby
2nd Maryland Brigade	Brigadier-General Mordecai Gist (500)
2nd Maryland Regiment	Lieutenant-Colonel John Eager Howard
4th Maryland Regiment	Colonel Josiah Carvel Hall
6th Maryland Regiment	Lieutenant-Colonel Benjamin Ford
The Delaware Regiment (brigaded with the 2nd Maryland Brigade) Lieutenant-Colonel Joseph Vaughan (280)	
Armand's Legion of Horse and Foot	Lieutenant-Colonel Charles Tuffin Armand
Cavalry (60)	
1st Troop Dragoons	Lieutenant-Colonel Richard Heard
2nd Troop Dragoons	Captain Henry Bedkin
3rd Troop Dragoons	Captain Jerome le Brun de Bellecour
Infantry	
Corps of German Volunteers	Captain Jost Driesbach (40)
Chasseur Company	Captain Jacob Baner (20)
Major Nelson's Regiment of Virginia State Cavalry	Captain Edmund Read (62)
1st Troop	Captain Edmund Read
2nd Troop	Captain Martin Armand Vogluson
3rd Troop	Captain Charles Fierer
South Carolina Volunteer Mounted Infantry	Major Thomas Pinckney (70)
Continental Artillery	Colonel Charles Harrison
1st Continental Artillery Regiment of Virginia	Captain William Meredith
2-pdrs (2)	
1st Maryland Continental Artillery Company	Captain Richard Dorsey
3-pdrs (2)	
2nd and 3rd Maryland Artillery	Captain Anthony Singleton
6-pdrs (4)	
Light Infantry	Major John Armstrong
Lieutenant-Colonel Porterfield's State Detachment	Captain Thomas H. Drew
North Carolina Troops	Major John Armstrong
North Carolina Militia	Brigadier-General Richard Caswell (1,200–1,500)
1st Brigade	Brigadier-General John Butler
2nd Brigade	Brigadier-General Griffith Rutherford
3rd Brigade	Brigadier-General Isaac Gregory
Virginia Militia 700	Brigadier-General Edward Stevens
South Carolina Militia	Captain Benjamin Carter

THE SIEGE OF CHARLESTON

Despite his generally pessimistic outlook, Clinton appears to have been energized by planning for an active operation against Charleston. There were several reasons to explain his improved mood at the time. First of all, he was returning to the site of a previous failure, his disastrous 'southern expedition' of 1776 in which he had failed to capture the unfinished fort on Sullivan's Island, which guarded the entrance to Charleston harbour. Clinton was able to nurture a grudge for years and the chance of making amends for this blot on his copybook was tantalizing. Secondly, Clinton had a flair for planning offensives. He had demonstrated time and time again during his period as Howe's second in command that he had bold ideas on how to approach the rebellion. Howe had refused to listen but now, after a frustrating hiatus, Clinton was able to return to the planning table to plot a major operation.

There was plenty to consider. Taking Charleston would be a major undertaking and one of the challenges presented was strikingly similar to one faced by the British in New York three years earlier; in both cases there was a significant natural obstacle to overcome. At New York it had been the heavily wooded slopes of the Gowanus Heights along Long Island, through

The palmetto and earth walls of the still-unfinished fort on Sullivan's Island had defied the Royal Navy in 1776, and it was hoped the defiance would continue in 1780. (Anne S. K. Brown Military Collection)

which there were only a few easy routes. At Charleston there was the bar, a sandbank that blocked the entrance to the harbour and was easily passable through only a few channels. The Americans also faced many of the same questions that had tormented Washington in 1776. Charleston would be difficult to defend without substantial naval forces, but unless a French fleet arrived, or help could be summoned from the Spanish, the Royal Navy was likely to enjoy a clear superiority. The same pressure from Congress that had forced Washington to defend New York had also been applied to Lincoln at Charleston. He felt obligated to defend the city, even though he realized that preserving his army was perhaps the most important service he could render to the rebel cause. Washington had proved able to extricate his army from near-certain destruction at New York. Lincoln would need to play his game very carefully if he was to do the same.

While planning his operation, Clinton received news of a number of French vessels wintering in the Chesapeake. Arbuthnot was eager to capture or destroy what he believed to be eight French warships but Clinton, believing the force to be far less significant (it was actually a 74-gun ship and two frigates), did not want to be distracted from his primary goal. Although he wanted eventually to establish a British base in the Chesapeake, both to act as a safe haven for loyalists in the area and to interfere with the Americans' ability to support their southern troops, he was more concerned with the approach of severe winter weather and wanted to get to Charleston as quickly as possible. The French ships were left in peace, at Yorktown.

Clinton boarded ship in New York at noon on Christmas Day 1779. His army, little short of 8,000 men, was ready to take the war to the rebels once more. Sailing with Clinton were the 7th, 23rd, 33rd, 63rd and 64th regiments, along with part of the 71st, two battalions of light infantry, two battalions of grenadiers, a squadron of the 17th Light Dragoons, Lord Cathcart's Legion, the New York Volunteers, the American Volunteers and the Royal Artillery. Hessian forces comprised the Regiment von Huyn, 250 Jägers and four grenadier battalions.

The extensive waterways surrounding Charleston presented a similar challenge to that posed by Manhattan in 1776. Britain also had to contend with enemy naval forces and a treacherous sandbar blocking entrance to the harbour. (Library of Congress)

Clinton's forebodings about the onset of bad weather proved justified – almost immediately after sailing, the fleet was hit by a series of violent winter storms that turned the voyage into a nightmare. As well as dragging the journey out to almost a month, a transport ship, *Russia Merchant*, was lost, taking with it most of Clinton's siege train. The army's horses were also mostly lost and one transport, carrying Hessian troops, was dismasted and blown across the Atlantic to England. Clinton, a poor sailor at the best of times, must have found the voyage tortuous, but the battered fleet finally began to assemble off the coast of Georgia at the end of January. Faced with making a decision on how to proceed to Charleston, Clinton was understandably reluctant to return to sea, but he finally accepted there was no reasonable alternative and, after detaching a small force under Brigadier-General James Paterson (including the cavalry, with a mission to secure remounts), the fleet set sail once more.

THE CHARLESTON DEFENCES

The Americans had been well aware of British designs in the south and had been taking steps to strengthen the city of Charleston against the expected assault. The fourth-largest city in the colonies at the time, Charleston was home to 12,000 people, about half of whom were slaves. On 11 November 1779, Washington had been ordered to send two regiments of North Carolina Continentals to Charleston; 828 of them set out on 23 November. Washington also decided that 2,500 Virginia Continentals along with 125 light dragoons under William Washington (a distant cousin of the American commander-in-chief) should head south as well. The problem was that the presence of Royal Navy ships made it too risky to send these reinforcements by sea, so they were forced to make a gruelling march to reach Charleston. The North Carolina Continentals did not reach their destination until 3 March 1780, while the Virginians (who set out on 12 December) did not arrive until 7 April, and less than 800 of them at that, the remainder having stopped in Virginia to await new uniforms.

A South Carolina $60 bill. De Kalb commented, 'A hat costs four hundred dollars, boots the same, and everything else in proportion… Money scatters like chaff before the wind, and expenses almost double from one day to the next.' (Author's collection)

Lincoln had six South Carolina Continental regiments with him in Charleston, but these had suffered such attrition during the war that they were reorganized into three infantry regiments and a fourth artillery regiment, numbering just 800 men in total. Lincoln also had the 600-strong Charleston Regiment of Militia and the 270-strong Charleston Battalion of Artillery. Lincoln requested reinforcements from North Carolina, supplies from Virginia and called in two detachments of Virginia troops (numbering 350 men) from Augusta. North Carolina militia did arrive on 10 February, but only to the number of 1,248. Recognizing the seriousness of his situation, Lincoln favoured arming slaves to form several battalions, but slave-owners could not be persuaded – not only were they unwilling to put their valuable possessions in harm's way, they also had a dread of seeing their slaves armed. Lincoln also had doubts over the ability of back-country militia to get into the city. He expected the British to try to distract them with operations inland and also had to contend with a smallpox outbreak in Charleston. Although Lincoln claimed it had run its course by March, many still feared coming into the city and catching the disease.

One area where Lincoln was to enjoy a superiority, at least during the early stages of the campaign, was in cavalry. While British cavalrymen scoured the countryside to find fresh horses, a 400-strong American force was able to operate with great freedom. Congress had also sought to offset the Royal Navy's supremacy as much as possible, sending three frigates to Charleston. *Providence*, *Boston* and *Queen of France* brought the total naval force at Lincoln's disposal to six frigates, a sloop and two brigs, under the command of Whipple. They were no match for the ships of the line in the British fleet, but it was hoped that these behemoths would not be able to play an active role in the operations around Charleston because of their inability to cross the bar. The few ships at the Americans' disposal were stationed inside the bar – Lincoln intended them to prevent British ships from getting through any of the channels, but he was not the only commander to have to deal with a non-cooperative naval counterpart during the siege of Charleston.

In 1776, the only defensive work Charleston had needed was the fort on Sullivan's Island. Now completed, and named Fort Moultrie after its gallant commander from three years previously, the fort housed 40 guns, with Colonel Charles Cotesworth Pinckney commanding. The city itself occupied the bottom end of a long peninsula, with fortifications along the 'neck' having originally been built in the 1750s. These defences had been strengthened during the British approach to the city the previous year and were now augmented still further. By the time British siegeworks opened, the defences were formidable. The main line of defensive works, comprising a chain of redoubts and

Charles Cotesworth Pinckney, commanding at Fort Moultrie in 1780, also took part in the defence of Charleston in 1776. After the war he twice ran for President, but was badly defeated on each occasion. (Anne S. K. Brown Military Collection)

batteries linked by parapets, was supplemented by a 6ft ditch immediately in front of it, measuring between 8ft and 12ft in width. At the bottom of this ditch were two lines of palisades (sharp wooden stakes driven into the ground) to impede the progress of an attacker. In front of the ditch was a double line of abatis, formed both from felled trees with sharpened limbs pointing towards the attacker, and manufactured *chevaux de frise*, made up of solid pieces of wood studded with sharp stakes. The medieval flavour of the American defences was completed by a flooded ditch, or canal, 18ft across and up to 8ft in depth. Pits were dug between the canal and the double line of abatis. The defences across the neck housed 79 field pieces, a howitzer and a few mortars and the area to their front had been cleared as much as possible, with trees and even houses levelled. Behind the main line, a redoubt known as the 'hornwork' offered a potential strongpoint into which the rebels could retreat if driven from their main works. Further defensive works stretched along the riversides around the city, offering no resistance to a land-based advance but hopefully deterring British naval forces from penetrating into the Ashley or Cooper rivers.

As daunting as these defences were, the chances were they would never actually have to repel an attacking force. Siegecraft had developed to the level of a science and the remorseless process of constructing approaches and trenches from which to bombard the defences was extremely difficult to resist. Usually, when the critical point came, a defending garrison would recognize the futility of further resistance and no assault would be needed. Before testing this theory on the American defenders, however, Clinton faced the difficult task of moving his army into position. His chosen landing point was Simmons Island, which was far enough from Charleston to let him land his men in safety, but entailed a lengthy trek to the Charleston neck. The lack of horses would make the work harder, as would the need for naval cooperation – Clinton would need Arbuthnot to get ships over the bar in order to ferry the army across the Ashley and onto the neck. Aware that the Americans seemed determined to defend the city, he also called for reinforcements from von Knyphausen in New York and called Paterson's small corps back.

Lincoln, after consulting with his officers, decided it was too risky to try to confront Clinton away from the security of the defensive works, so he kept the bulk of his army within the lines and left it to his cavalry to harass the British advance as best they could. Clinton crossed the bulk of his men to James Island on 24 February, and on 3 March he was resupplied with artillery and entrenching tools by the navy (he had also called for artillery from St Augustine and the Bahamas). This gave Clinton his siege train, but left Arbuthnot in an understandable state of anxiety over his weakened ships – the appearance of a French fleet was always to be feared. Spanish intervention, however, was not to be a factor. An approach from the Americans to

Benjamin Lincoln called upon William Moultrie, as one of his most experienced officers, to take charge of the defensive works protecting Charleston during the siege. (Anne S. K. Brown Military Collection)

Spanish forces on Cuba had been rejected in February. On 10 March, Clinton made a move to open up the Ashley to British shipping, building a battery on Fenwick's Point that could threaten both Charleston itself and American ships. A second battery on the same site effectively allowed Arbuthnot access to the Ashley, if only he could get his ships across the bar.

The bar, several miles long, was not to be taken lightly, reducing the depth of water to as little as 3ft in places. Buoys marking the several safe passages had been removed by the Americans, but by 9 March the British had managed to mark the Ship Channel. This passage was not deep enough for Arbuthnot to hazard any of his four ships of the line (*Europe*, *Russell*, *Raisonable* and *Robust*) and even his smaller warships were at risk, forcing Arbuthnot to make the decision to lighten them by removing guns. To be certain of safely passing the bar, Arbuthnot also waited for a flood tide. How vulnerable the British ships would have been in their lightened state (as well as lessening their ability to defend themselves, the loss of guns also significantly altered their sailing characteristics) became a moot point, because Whipple refused to contest the British passing of the bar, grouping his ships instead under the protective guns of Fort Moultrie. On 20 March, Arbuthnot ordered seven ships through the Ship Channel. All made it safely into the reassuringly named Five Fathom Hole and Whipple withdrew his ships still farther, into the Cooper.

Everything appeared to be running smoothly for the British, but two elements were emerging that would make life difficult for Clinton. The day before Arbuthnot got his ships over the bar, Clinton received a letter from Germain. Clinton's latest request to resign his post had been denied. This news prompted a remarkable response from Cornwallis. As Clinton's second in command, he had been consulted extensively on every move made by the British army up to that point. In fact, Clinton claimed that he had allowed Cornwallis's opinion to take precedence as much as possible because of the likelihood of his taking over command of the army at any time. Upon hearing that he would not be taking over, Cornwallis apparently gave the matter some thought for a few days and then declared that he no longer wished to be consulted on operational decisions. Clinton had a right to feel aggrieved at this – his second in command ought of course to have made himself available as a sounding board. There was a personal element as well, however; Clinton was hurt that the army was so obviously fond of Cornwallis and had appeared to be happy at the thought of his taking over. Cornwallis's own obvious willingness to take his place had also touched a nerve.

As well as the deterioration in his relationship with Cornwallis, Clinton was about to start butting heads with Arbuthnot who, in passing the bar, had just made his last major contribution to the siege of Charleston. As the weeks passed, Clinton was forced to operate without the close support of two men he should have been able to rely upon and Arbuthnot's uncooperativeness in particular might have cost him his prize. Clinton wanted to capture or destroy the entire rebel army – he recognized the importance of Charleston as a base for British reconquest of the Carolinas, but he also recognized what a hollow victory it would be if the American army escaped to act as a rallying point for rebels in the region. By far the easiest way of ensuring that nobody escaped Charleston would be to complete the investiture of the city and by far the easiest way to achieve that would be for land forces to block off the

Charleston neck at the same time as Arbuthnot moved ships into the Cooper to cut off the rebels' line of retreat. That was to become a sticking point, as Arbuthnot was unhappy at the risk to his shipping of such a move. For now, Clinton made use of the assistance that Arbuthnot was willing to offer. The admiral provided 75 flatboats and crews, sailing them through Wappoo Cut and up the Ashley, and on 29 March the bulk of Clinton's army crossed the Ashley in three waves, landing at Fuller's Plantation. By the evening, British forces were within 6 miles of Charleston.

Lincoln's response was limited – he formed a small light infantry battalion under Lieutenant-Colonel John Laurens and posted it outside the main defensive line. However, when the British pushed forward on 30 March, Laurens was ordered to withdraw to the lines (he had wanted to stand and fight and had even called for artillery support). The following day, entrenching tools and artillery were ferried across the Ashley and the day after that, on 1 April, a body of 3,000 men (half labourers and half a protective screen of infantry) began work on three redoubts at a range of about 1,000 yards from the Charleston defences. The siege had begun.

The relationship between Abraham Whipple and Benjamin Lincoln was in some respects similar to that between Arbuthnot and Clinton – neither general could get his naval counterpart to cooperate as fully as he would have liked. (Image Courtesy of U.S. Naval Academy Museum)

THE SIEGE OF CHARLESTON

There was a certain inevitability to the events that followed, but that does not mean there was no way out for the Americans. As long as an escape route was open across the Cooper, they could abandon the city at any moment. Lincoln was no fool and he understood that a successful resistance was unlikely, but while the Cooper offered an exit strategy, he was prepared to allow events to take their course. In any case, simply by holding up the British he felt that he could serve the patriot cause.

British progress was initially swift. On the first night of siegeworks they threw up three redoubts, following the plan submitted by Major James Moncrief (there were to be six redoubts in the first parallel). It took a day for the Americans to position guns to resist, but by the evening of 2 April they were firing on the newly constructed British works. On 3 April they lobbed an estimated 300 solid cannonballs at the redoubts, which by then had been strengthened. The American fire apparently did no damage, but that story would change as the British inched nearer and the range lessened. That night, the British built redoubt No. 6, only 400–500 yards from the right of the American line, prompting a furious response from the defenders. Clinton,

The capture of Charleston

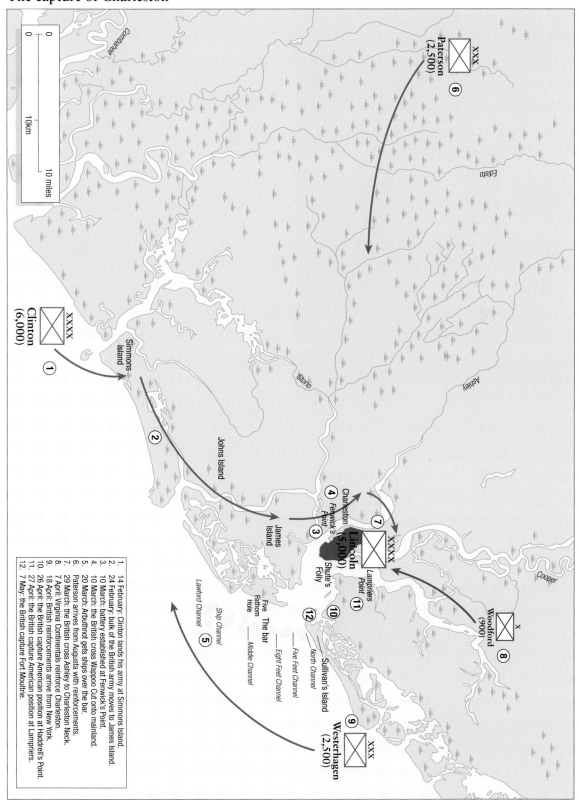

Scale: 0 10 miles / 0 10km

Labels on map:
- Combahee
- Paterson (2,500) xxx ⑥
- Edisto
- Clinton (6,000) xxxx ①
- Simmons Island ②
- Johns Island
- Stono
- James Island
- Ashley
- Charleston ④ Fenwick's Point ③
- Lincoln (5,000) xxxx ⑦
- Lampriers Point ⑪
- Shute's Folly ⑫
- Lawford Channel ⑤
- Ship Channel
- The bar Fathom Hole
- Five Feet Channel
- Eight Feet Channel
- North Channel
- Sullivan's Island ⑩
- Woodford (900) x ⑧
- Cooper
- Westerhagen (2,500) xxx ⑨

1. 14 February: Clinton lands his army at Simmons Island.
2. 24 February: bulk of the British army moves to James Island.
3. 10 March: battery established at Fenwick's Point.
4. 10 March: the British cross Wappoo Cut onto mainland.
5. 20 March: Arbuthnot gets ships over the bar.
6. Paterson arrives from Augusta with reinforcements.
7. 29 March: the British cross Ashley to Charleston Neck.
8. 7 April: Virginia Continentals reinforce Charleston.
9. 18 April: British reinforcements arrive from New York.
10. 26 April: the British capture American position at Haddrell's Point.
11. 27 April: the British capture American position at Lampriers.
12. 7 May: the British capture Fort Moultrie.

33

Arbuthnot was not the first (or the last) admiral to run into rough seas with Henry Clinton. Sir Peter Parker, commanding naval forces during the Southern Expedition of 1776, had been hounded by Clinton for years afterwards. (Anne S. K. Brown Military Collection)

concerned that the Americans might try to storm the redoubt, posted 100 Hessian Jägers there under the hugely experienced Ewald. On 7 April the British completed their first parallel – all that was required now was for artillery to be placed within the line and they would be able to reply to the American guns.

There was better news for Lincoln on the same day – 737 Virginia Continentals, under William Woodford, landed at Gadsden's Wharf. Not only were they good troops, their arrival also demonstrated that the Americans still enjoyed communications with the outside world via the Cooper. In fact, they were to receive supplies for a considerable time to come, and the largely one-way traffic at least theoretically proved that an evacuation was still an option. Ewald wrote of his disappointment that the Americans had been able to reinforce their garrison, but Clinton was pleased, seeing it as increasing the scale of his ultimate victory, if only he could prevent the rebel army from escaping. Clinton was making solid progress on his side of the two-pronged strategy, having sealed off the Charleston neck, but Arbuthnot was proving unwilling to risk his ships in the Cooper. Two potential obstacles concerned the admiral. The guns of Fort Moultrie demanded respect, and the Americans had also constructed a boom across the deeper part of the entrance to the Cooper. This boom, anchored by scuttled ships including the *Queen of France*, blocked off the passage between Charleston and Shute's Folly. A second passage (Hog Island Channel) was left open, but this was shallow and Arbuthnot was concerned his warships might not be able to navigate it safely. Whipple, with the remainder of his naval force, was now situated behind the boom. The Charleston garrison also benefited from the scuttling of the ships – it freed up around 1,000 men and 150 guns for the town's defences.

Clinton had been pressing Arbuthnot to sail past Fort Moultrie and the slow-moving admiral finally complied on 8 April. His fears proved to have been unfounded. Nine warships and three transports got safely past the thundering guns of the fort, while a single transport ran aground and was burnt by the British. The garrison of Fort Moultrie had suffered 27 casualties in the action and the British fleet was now in Charleston harbour. Clinton and Arbuthnot held a conference on 9 April, at which Clinton made it clear that he wanted Arbuthnot to take his chances in Hog Island Channel and complete the investiture of Charleston. There was a chance that closing the back door would force the rebels to surrender and Clinton was beginning to worry over the length of time it was taking his men to prepare batteries in the first parallel. Having lost their horses, the British were having to manhandle guns and ammunition through marshy ground, made all the worse by heavy rains. It was exhausting work and progress was slow. As if anticipating the difficulties he would encounter in getting Arbuthnot to budge, Clinton also ordered a body of 1,500 men, under Lieutenant-Colonel James Webster, over to the east side of the Cooper. If the investiture of the city could not be completed by naval forces, it might still be achieved on land.

On 10 April, Clinton offered terms to the garrison of Charleston. Lincoln rejected them out of hand. Although aware of his perilous situation there seemed little urgency at that moment, but the picture changed dramatically three days later; British batteries in the first parallel were finally taking shape. During a meeting with his officers on 13 April, at which the possibility of evacuating the army was discussed, the British took up the challenge thrown down by the rebel artillery in their defensive line. Guns (most of them 24-pdrs), howitzers and mortars began a day-long bombardment of the rebel defences and the city itself. With the bombardment including 'hot shot', several buildings in Charleston were set on fire, provoking a furious response from Clinton, who raged against the barbarity of setting fire to a city he wanted to capture intact. Although Clinton's stance was undoubtedly humane, his gunners would have been frustrated at being prevented from ending operations in one or two days.

On the same day, the Americans proved they could still evacuate by sending Governor Rutledge and several invalids (including Francis Marion, who was to enjoy considerable success as a commander of militia) out of the city. Lincoln was aware of the critical importance of keeping this lifeline open and ordered construction of a defensive work at Lampriers Point to keep British ships out of the Cooper, arming it with six 18-pounders from the now redundant Fort Moultrie. It was a small gesture, but one that would have a significant impact. At the same time that Lincoln sought to strengthen his grip on the east bank of the Cooper, the British were seeking to weaken it. British cavalry forces, having found new horses in the South Carolina countryside, made their first contribution to the campaign. Tarleton, along with Ferguson's American Volunteers, destroyed a rebel force under Colonel Washington at Monck's Corner during a daring night attack on 14 April. American losses were severe – 15 dead, 63 captured and as many as 400 horses commandeered by the British, who also took 40 wagonloads of supplies. A militia force was also scattered as a secondary part of the same action, during which British losses numbered one officer and two men. Lincoln accordingly ordered his men east of the Cooper to concentrate at Lampriers Point. Tarleton, at this point, declared that the investiture of the city was now complete, but that was not the case – work still needed to be done.

It was becoming increasingly likely that the work would have to proceed without the assistance of Arbuthnot, whom Clinton could not convince to move. He would later write: 'I therefore made use of every argument I could think of to impress the Admiral with conviction of its importance, but I could only obtain from him reiterated promises that he would very shortly comply

John Laurens was an aggressive officer who wanted to take the fight to the British when they arrived on Charleston Neck, but Benjamin Lincoln kept him on a tight rein. (Author's collection)

THE BOMBARDMENT OF CHARLESTON (PP. 36–37)

After a drawn-out, cautious approach to Charleston, Henry Clinton was ready to increase the pressure on the town by the middle of April. Initially stymied by the loss of his siege train during the voyage from New York, he scraped together enough heavy artillery to stock the first parallel of his siege lines and a day-long bombardment commenced at 10am on 13 April.

Ironically, the American commander, Benjamin Lincoln, was in conference with his officers on the possibility of surrendering the city when the firing commenced.

Prior to this, the British had already closed off the Ashley River with the construction of a battery at Fenwick's Point (now Albemarle Point) (**1**). On 11 March a house had been burned down to give the battery an uninterrupted view over the river and the battery had been thrown up overnight. It was supplied with five cannon (three 32-pdrs and two 24-pdrs) and a howitzer, on 12 March.

The battery proved its worth immediately, repelling two rebel galleys, the *Lee* and the *Bretigny* and also engaging a brig, the *Notre Dame*, which unwisely strayed too close. The American ships were able to withdraw safely on each occasion, but the Ashley was now out of bounds.

The battery on Fenwick's point would have enjoyed a fine view of the artillery duel between the British and American guns on 13 April and would have taken part itself (the battery was within range of the city even though its main purpose was to keep shipping out of the Ashley) (**2**).

Part of the city of Charleston was set on fire during the bombardment, but Clinton quickly ordered that heated shot should not be used. Also visible along the Charleston skyline is the tower of St Michael's church (**3**). This prominent building was used as a vantage point by the Americans throughout the siege, allowing them to keep track of British movements, although they ultimately proved unable to resist them.

with my desire – notwithstanding which I had the mortification to be disappointed, as no attempt was *ever* made by him to send ships into the Cooper to end the siege.' Clinton came to view Arbuthnot as not only uncooperative, but untrustworthy and two-faced as well. This was almost certainly casting the admiral in too dark a light, but, together with Clinton's falling out with Cornwallis, it presented the commander-in-chief with a problem. Fortunately, a solution, or at least a way around the problem, soon presented itself. On 18 April, the reinforcements Clinton had called up from New York arrived, comprising the 42nd Regiment, the Queen's Rangers, the Prince of Wales Regiment, the Volunteers of Ireland and the Hessian Regiment von Ditfurth. The total, more than 2,500 men, gave Clinton options. First of all, he was able to beef up the corps operating on the east of the Cooper, giving them a chance of sealing the Americans' escape route without the cooperation of Arbuthnot. Secondly, the increased size of the corps made it a suitable command for Cornwallis, and Clinton must have felt relief at getting his second in command out of the way. Cornwallis was now commanding 2,300 men (the 23rd, the Volunteers of Ireland and the South Carolina Royalists augmenting the men already with Webster). Clinton asked Cornwallis to look into the possibility of attacking the American position at Lampriers Point and a new work at Haddrell's Point. This second work, commenced on 22 April, had become yet another reason why Arbuthnot was unwilling to risk a passage of the Hog Island Channel.

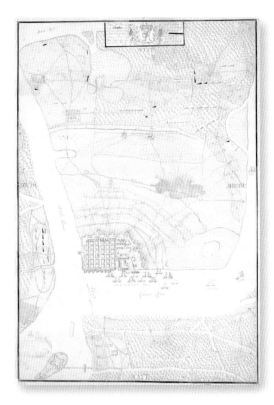

A contemporary map of the siege of Charleston shows how the city was nestled in the tip of the peninsula, but grossly exaggerates the extent of the British siege lines. (Library of Congress)

Clinton could now see real signs of progress. An approach trench for the second parallel had been started even before the guns had been positioned in the first. Interestingly, this trench was constructed in a straight line, rather than the zigzag that would normally have been expected. Moncrief, architect of the British plans, believed the rebels were not a significant enough opponent to merit the slower but safer method of a zigzagging approach. A redoubt was constructed on the night of 9 April, 150 yards in front of the first parallel. By 13 April the approach had been extended to within 750ft of the canal and it was here that ground was broken for the second parallel. As the distance between the antagonists decreased, the Americans constructed a redoubt on their right in advance of their main line, in which they could post soldiers. Rifle fire was soon to add its own distinctive noise to the battlefield and the toll of death and injury on both sides was about to increase. The American response to the opening of the second parallel forced Moncrief to open another section farther to the left of the American lines. On the night of 17 April, the two sections joined and the second parallel was complete. Clinton placed the elite troops of his army, the Hessian Jägers, in the new trench to counteract the American riflemen and a deadly duel started. British and Hessian troops also started to use small mortars, 'coehorns', as they got closer to the rebel lines, the Americans responding with grapeshot. For all the scientific principles employed for the construction and defence of siegeworks, it was becoming a hellish world for the men actually in the trenches.

BRITISH UNITS
1. 7th Regiment
2. 71st Regiment
3. 33rd Regiment
4. Hessian Grenadiers
5. British Grenadiers
6. Artillery Park
7. 42nd Regiment
8. Light Infantry
9. Hessian Jägers

xxxx

CLINTON

▼ **EVENTS**

1. British construct a battery at Fenwick's Point on 11 March to protect the army from American naval activity on the Ashley River.

2. After crossing the Ashley on 29 March, British troops march on Charleston.

3. Two days later, artillery is crossed at Gibbes' Landing.

4. Work on the first parallel is opened on 1 April. It is completed six days later.

5. The American garrison is reinforced by the arrival of nearly 800 Virginia Continentals on 8 April, proving that an escape over the Cooper River is still possible.

6. Sunken ships form a boom between Charleston and Shute's Folly.

7. British reinforcements numbering more than 2,500 arrive from New York, including the 42nd Regiment.

8. The third parallel is started on 21 April and the defensive canal constructed by the Americans is breached on 1 May. Artillery is moved into the third parallel on 1 May, setting the stage for a final assault of the city.

9. Lincoln accepts Clinton's terms for surrender on 11 May.

THE SIEGE OF CHARLESTON

14 February to 11 May 1780. With the American commander, Benjamin Lincoln, refusing to leave his defensive positions, the British gradually tightened the noose around Charleston until surrender was inevitable.

Note: Gridlines are shown at intervals of 1km

COOPER RIVER

LINCOLN

AMERICAN UNITS
A. North Carolina Continentals
B. South Carolina Continentals
C. Light Infantry Corps
D. 2nd Virginia Brigade
E. 1st Virginia Brigade (arrived 8 April)
F. Charleston Militia Brigade
G. North & South Carolina militia

CHARLESTON

ASHLEY RIVER

N

An effective depiction of the British lines as the siege progressed, but the bearskins worn by these unfortunate soldiers would have proved intolerable during the draining, humid weather experienced by besieger and besieged alike. (Anne S. K. Brown Military Collection)

Lincoln's situation had been complicated by the fact that many of his North Carolina militia had left Charleston on the expiration of their enlistments at the end of March. He had asked the colony to make good the numbers, requesting 2,500 men, but was told to expect only 300. When the British started their approach trench for the third parallel, Lincoln realized that time was running out. On 20 April, he again called his officers together and it appears there was a strong possibility of the Continental troops being evacuated. The furious interjection of the Lieutenant Governor, Christopher Gadsden, was critical. Appalled at the possibility of the city being given up without a fight, he brought four other privy councillors to the meeting and demanded that resistance be maintained. Thomas Ferguson, one of the privy councillors, is reported to have threatened to open the city gates to the British so that they could attack the departing Continentals, if the decision was taken to abandon the city. This extraordinary outburst took evacuation off the table for the time being, but the following day Lincoln requested terms from Clinton. As the letter was addressed only to Clinton, the British commander reproved Lincoln, explaining that he should have addressed it to Arbuthnot as well. Lincoln's response, that Arbuthnot 'was so far off he did not consider him as forming part of the siege', may have brought a rueful smile to Clinton's face.

Lincoln's terms were never likely to have been accepted, involving as they did a 36-hour window for troops to be evacuated followed by a ten-day head start before Clinton started a pursuit. Clinton, bemused by the American request, instead offered his original terms once more. By 10.30 that evening the failure to come to an agreement was made clear by the British guns, which recommenced their bombardment of the city. An estimated 20 civilians were killed during the siege, and something like 30 houses destroyed, but the toll could undoubtedly have been much worse had Clinton turned his gunners loose.

The third parallel was now under way and time was running out for both sides. This final parallel was also constructed in two sections, although this time they did not meet. The British were 800ft from the main rebel line and Clinton began to consider the grim possibility that the Americans might actually force him to storm their defences. The outcome of an assault was perhaps not greatly in doubt, but he could ill afford the inevitable casualties that would result. Further frustration came from Cornwallis, who declared the American position at Lampriers too strong to assault, and Arbuthnot, who still refused to make a move up the Cooper. However, the works that had caused Arbuthnot so much consternation, Fort Moultrie, Lampriers Point and Haddrell's Point, were all about to fall.

FINAL MOVES

One of the principal ways of defending a siege was the 'sally', where the garrison would send a small force to attack a section of the enemy trenches. As well as instilling panic and hopefully inflicting a few casualties, there was also the possibility of spiking enemy guns and putting them out of action, at least for a while. Surprisingly, the Americans had made no use of this tactic, but on the night of 23–24 April, that changed. A party of 200 South Carolina and Virginia Continentals attacked the third parallel, killing eight British and Hessian soldiers and taking 12 prisoners. Although American losses were light, with only one man killed, that was no consolation to William Moultrie – it was his brother, Thomas, who died. The following night, obviously unnerved by the American attack, a panic erupted in the third parallel and British troops in the second and first lines actually shot and killed several of their own men in the darkness, thinking it was another American attack.

On the east bank of the Cooper, however, things were going better for the British. On 26 April Cornwallis captured the three-gun position at Haddrell's Point, the Americans evacuating without a fight as the British approached. The next night, the garrison at Lampriers, mistakenly believing it was being attacked, left precipitously. Four 18-pdrs, as well as several smaller guns, were left behind. On the morning of 28 April the Americans in Charleston could clearly see the British flag flying over Lampriers. The Cooper was now open. Arbuthnot, however, chose to view the fall of the two American positions as a completion of the investiture of the city; naval intervention was no longer needed, in his opinion. It would not be fair to ignore a minor contribution from the admiral – marines and sailors from his ships captured Fort Moultrie on 7 May. Again, the garrison surrendered without resistance and the fort had already outlived its usefulness, but as a symbol of Charleston's resistance in 1776, its loss was a severe blow to the morale of the city. The fall of Fort Moultrie completed the reduction of American forces east of the Cooper. The day before it fell, Tarleton had struck again, wiping out a cavalry force at Lenud's Ferry. As many as 30 Americans were killed in the action, with 67 captured. Tarleton's men also captured 100 horses.

Despite these positive developments, the likelihood was growing that an assault of the rebel defences would be required. The rebel canal had been breached on 1 May and was steadily draining. In planning for the assault, Clinton counted on support from Arbuthnot, who would hopefully tie up rebel gunners on the shoreline to prevent them from resisting the storming of the lines. Clinton perhaps should have known better by now. Having initially promised to offer fire support during an assault, Arbuthnot had second

Nicknamed the 'Swamp Fox', Francis Marion (shown here wrapped in a blanket as his men cross the Pee Dee River) became a real thorn in the British side after he was evacuated from Charleston during the siege. (Anne S. K. Brown Military Collection)

thoughts. On 4 May he wrote to the general: 'I confess it would be against my judgement to place the ships against the enemy's batteries, circumstanced as they are, merely for a diversion.' A no-doubt fuming Clinton would not have been mollified by the assistance Arbuthnot went on to propose: 'When the moment arrives, the ships will at least by their movements indicate such a design to the enemy, which will answer the purpose you propose, that of keeping the men at the batteries on this side from opposing you.'

In a last-ditch effort to prevent the carnage of an assault, Clinton once more offered the Americans the same terms they had rejected previously. Lincoln received the offer on 8 May and there followed a prolonged period of haggling over terms, which must have been a welcome respite for the men in the lines. Agreement could not be reached on the status of the militia troops, or on what honours the garrison could claim upon surrendering the city – Lincoln asked that they be allowed to march out with colours unfurled and their band playing a British march, the traditional acknowledgement that they had staged a brave defence. Clinton did not think they had earned such an honour and also insisted on the militia being treated as prisoners of war, to be released on parole. At 9.00pm the following day negotiations broke down and the British guns opened up once more, with their heaviest bombardment of the siege to date. British approaches reached within 25ft of the main rebel line.

Remarkably, the end came when the American militia, having heard that its status was a stumbling block in negotiations, petitioned Lincoln to accept Clinton's terms. At the same time the civil authorities also lost their nerve. On 11 May they asked Lincoln to surrender, having refused to allow him to withdraw his army previously. Later that day, Lincoln accepted Clinton's terms.

The siege of Charleston had cost the lives of 99 British soldiers and sailors and 89 Americans. It had also cost Clinton the cooperation of two important officers, which would have serious consequences in the months to follow. For now, Clinton could bask in the glory of his greatest military success, indeed the greatest success enjoyed by the British during the entire war. As well as exorcizing the demons of 1776, Clinton had taken a big step towards a successful implementation of the southern strategy. 'Both the Carolinas are conquered in Charles Town,' he wrote. Subsequent events would prove him wrong – and it would not take long.

CAMDEN

Clinton's optimism regarding the state of affairs in the southern colonies was perhaps coloured by the realization that he would not be responsible for events that followed. During the siege, he had received news that a French fleet was on its way to North America and was expected to target New York. Just as had happened in the middle of operations against Charleston in 1776, Clinton suddenly felt an overwhelming urge to be back in New York. Before leaving, however, he put the second stage of the British strategy in motion.

Initially intent only on capturing Charleston, Clinton had been reluctant to call out loyalist support, asking those well disposed to the crown to remain peacefully in their homes until called upon. Now, with Charleston secured as a refuge for loyalists and with the rebel militia disarmed (although they had been allowed to return to their homes on parole), not to mention the almost complete destruction of Continental forces in the colony, Clinton felt able to make that call. On 22 May he handed Major Patrick Ferguson his official instructions as Inspector of Militia.

Ferguson was to attempt to enlist 'all the young or unmarried men of the provinces of Georgia and the two Carolinas … into companies consisting of from 50 to 100 men each and … form battalions consisting of from 6 to 12 companies each'. Independent companies were permissible where it was not easy to form battalions and each company was to have a lieutenant chosen

The Pringle mansion became headquarters for the British in occupied Charleston. The same house would later serve in the same capacity for Union troops during the American Civil War. (Anne S. K. Brown Military Collection)

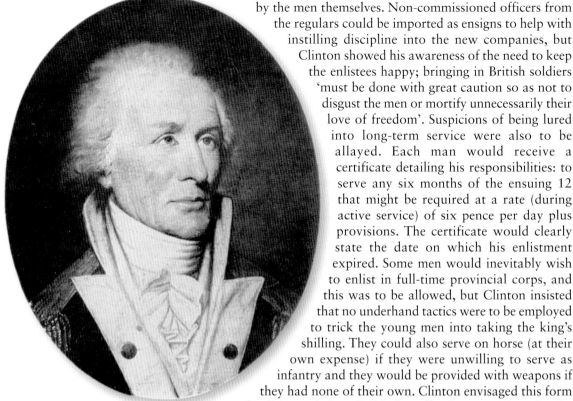

One of the leading militia commanders in the south, Thomas Sumter, found that he had to keep his men occupied or they would simply melt away. (Library of Congress)

by the men themselves. Non-commissioned officers from the regulars could be imported as ensigns to help with instilling discipline into the new companies, but Clinton showed his awareness of the need to keep the enlistees happy; bringing in British soldiers 'must be done with great caution so as not to disgust the men or mortify unnecessarily their love of freedom'. Suspicions of being lured into long-term service were also to be allayed. Each man would receive a certificate detailing his responsibilities: to serve any six months of the ensuing 12 that might be required at a rate (during active service) of six pence per day plus provisions. The certificate would clearly state the date on which his enlistment expired. Some men would inevitably wish to enlist in full-time provincial corps, and this was to be allowed, but Clinton insisted that no underhand tactics were to be employed to trick the young men into taking the king's shilling. They could also serve on horse (at their own expense) if they were unwilling to serve as infantry and they would be provided with weapons if they had none of their own. Clinton envisaged this form of enlistee as being eligible for offensive operations, but he also saw the need for local forces, made up of older men or those with families. These men would need to be ready only 'to assemble occasionally in their several districts', to respond to temporary crises.

These were the types of units that Britain would be relying upon to maintain order in the southern colonies, to enable the regular army to move on and continue the pacification of the region. It is worth considering the principal adversary such loyalist forces would face: the patriot militia of South Carolina. Although Lincoln had been disappointed in the lack of back-country militia that had come to his aid at Charleston (he estimated that no more than 300 had come to the city), he had perhaps misunderstood the fundamental qualities of the men in question. The back-country militia had still been performing worthwhile work, subduing loyalists in the region and securing the frontier. It could not, however, be viewed in any way as an organized force that could be depended upon from one month to the next, or expected to march and fight in different regions as required. These citizen soldiers did not have the luxury of leaving their homesteads for extended periods of time – their families required protection and their labour was the only thing that put food on the table. They therefore responded to a crisis in much the same way as an immune system responds to an infection. They could come together to deal with an invader who threatened their own homes and farms, but expecting them to march to defend other settlements was asking too much of them and they were also likely to struggle with offensive operations a long way from home. This is not to say that the South Carolina militia was unmotivated. Its pragmatic approach was a necessity if their families were to survive in a hard country. There was little concept of a colony- or country-wide cause; the focus was strictly on local concerns.

The fall of Charleston would put this focus under intense pressure. As British forces spread their control throughout the back-country, patriots were faced with a choice. They could either accept the offer of parole, or they could join larger bands of militia. Remaining in their homes and acting as occasional soldiers was no longer an option as loyalist strength responded to the presence of the British. Many men chose to take parole and remove themselves from the war, but many others gathered around charismatic leaders like Thomas Sumter, James Williams and Francis Marion. There was a remarkable level of freedom and democracy in such units. The men would feel free simply to walk home if they disagreed with a chosen course of action, and there would be no shame in this (equally importantly, with no Whig government in the region there would be nobody to impose any official punishment). Likewise, officers would consult with each other to settle on plans and whether or not to stand and fight at any particular time. The composition of these forces would shift constantly. A man might leave one unit and join another if the aims of that unit seemed a closer match to his own concerns, or he might simply go home to respond to a family emergency. If there appeared to be no pressing need for action a region might seem calm, but the appearance of a British or loyalist force could change the situation overnight. It presented the British with a problem, and one that they failed to get to grips with. Nor was the South Carolina militia the only adversary the British had to be wary of. Even before Charleston fell, a new American army was marching to dispute British control of the south.

Originally called 'Pine Tree Hill', Camden had been renamed in honour of Lord Camden, who was an outspoken supporter of the colonies in the struggle with Britain, going so far as to declare that resistance to tyranny was justified. (Library of Congress)

THE MOVE INTO THE BACK-COUNTRY

Following the fall of Charleston, Clinton ordered three columns of troops to move into the back-country to establish British control over the entire region. Augusta, Ninety Six and Camden were the chief targets, but smaller posts were also set up to protect lines of communication and to extend influence over as wide an area as possible. The back-country of South Carolina was a vast region, a mixture of plains and forest. There was abundant wildlife and the area was largely unaltered despite three decades of settlement, with two exceptions: both the bison and the elk had been hunted to extinction. The population was formed of scattered farms and settlements, with Scotch-Irish and Germans the two major ethnic groups. The fiery Scotch-Irish contrasted sharply with the calmer Germans in a region evocatively described by Ian Saberton as 'not a melting pot … more akin to the Tower of Babel'. It was a productive region, contributing something like 3,000 wagonloads of grain and meat per year to the colony's economy, which sits rather awkwardly with the accepted picture of the Scotch-Irish as disdainful of hard work.

The British faced a major problem in the fact that most of what passed for the local 'gentry', the larger and more influential landowners, were revolutionary in sentiment. Still, there were sufficient loyalists to make the British strategy seem feasible, although the clannish behaviour of the population, and the propensity for feuds and arguments to be carefully nurtured, made the region volatile. Saberton described it as 'a powder keg waiting to explode'. The British were about to provide a spark.

One of Clinton's three columns heading into the back-country was commanded by Cornwallis. As soon as Charleston had fallen, Cornwallis had written to Amherst in England, requesting to serve elsewhere. He made it clear that he would serve in any climate, suggesting that even the fever-ridden islands of the West Indies would be preferable to continuing to serve under Clinton. To Clinton himself, Cornwallis made the more diplomatic assertion that he would be happy to continue in the south while Clinton returned to New York. His position was understandable when it is considered that he would have been third in command in New York (under both Clinton and the Hessian general von Knyphausen), while he could command in the south. Clinton, for his part, was probably happy to have an easy way of distancing himself from what had become a troublesome subordinate, but he does not seem to have considered fully the implications of leaving the delicate southern strategy in the hands of an officer he no longer trusted.

Cornwallis, with 2,500 men, set out for Camden on 18 May. He moved up the east side of the Santee River while, for a time, Francis Lord Rawdon marched on the opposite side with part of the command. Rawdon in particular was unimpressed with the destination, believing Camden to be a poor strategic position, 'on the wrong side of the river and covering nothing'. Nevertheless, it was the most important town in the back-country, rivalled only by the settlement at Ninety Six, towards which Major Patrick Ferguson set off on 26 May. This second column, just 600 strong, reached its goal on 22 June, but Balfour already had misgivings. He had advised Clinton against giving the firebrand Ferguson

Francis, Lord Rawdon, was in the early years of what was to become a distinguished military career. At Camden he displayed many of the qualities that were to come to the fore in later years and he also performed well at the 'Second Battle of Camden' the following year. (Print Collection, Miriam and Ira D. Wallach Division of Arts, Prints and Photographs, The New York Public Library)

The British Legion, commanded by Banastre Tarleton, was a provincial force composed of both mounted troops and infantry. Foot soldiers would often ride 'doubled-up' with cavalrymen when in pursuit of an enemy. (Painting by Don Troiani)

responsibility for embodying militia units and confided in Cornwallis that he did not think the man trustworthy for the conduct of any plan at all. The relationship between Cornwallis and Balfour was strong and the two men regularly shared their dissatisfaction with others. Having less than complete faith in the man responsible for embodying loyalist militia units was not a good start to the British plan, but for now that concern could take a back seat while Cornwallis dealt with another, more pressing matter.

THE BATTLE OF WAXHAWS

Following the steady decline in regimental numbers, the Virginia regiments had been reorganized into three 'Detachments', combining the various regiments into units of between 250 and 350 men. The First and Second detachments had made it to Charleston in time to take part in the defence of the city but the Third, 350 men commanded by Colonel Abraham Buford, was still marching towards the city when it fell. On 6 May, a party of around 150 of Buford's command had watched from the opposite side of the Santee River as Tarleton's men destroyed the remaining American cavalry force at Lenud's Ferry and, with the back door to Charleston now closed, Buford had little option but to withdraw his men. Any relief they may have felt at avoiding adding their numbers to the British prisoner of war lists was not to last for long. Escorting the South Carolina Governor, John Rutledge, Buford headed for Camden, with a substantial head start on British forces. This small body of men, representing both the government in exile and the last vestiges of Continental forces in the colony, was a tempting target when Cornwallis learned that they were likewise heading for Camden, but the ten-day head start made the British general cautious. He was willing to give Tarleton a chance, but made it clear that the cavalry commander had discretion to call off the pursuit if he thought it was futile.

Tarleton would have had no hope of catching the retreating rebels if he had not replaced his inferior horses with the fine mounts of the American cavalry following the actions at Monck's Corner and Lenud's Ferry (the latter of which, ironically, some of Buford's men had witnessed). With 40 men of the 17th Light Dragoons, 130 British Legion cavalry and 100 British Legion infantry (mounted), Tarleton set off on 27 May. A single 3-pdr gun accompanied him. Tarleton set such a ferocious pace that his men reached Camden the following day, having covered 60 miles on a road now spattered with collapsed horses, worn out from their exertions (remounts were found en route, when necessary). At Camden, Tarleton learned that Buford had been at Rugeley's Mills on the 26th and at 2.00am on the 29th, having given his men and horses a few precious

Tarleton's letter to Abraham Buford was intended to bluff the American into surrendering, offering terms similar to those accepted by the garrison at Charleston. The letter ended with a dark warning, stating that if Buford did not accept the terms, 'the blood be upon your head'. (Print Collection, Miriam and Ira D. Wallach Division of Arts, Prints and Photographs, The New York Public Library)

hours to recover, he renewed the pursuit. At Rugeley's Mills the British learned that the 350 Continentals were a mere 20 miles away and Tarleton dispatched a rider to try to bluff Buford into surrendering. The summons inflated Tarleton's numbers to 700 and also claimed that Cornwallis was within striking range with reinforcements. Buford refused to be tricked into halting to consider Tarleton's terms, but he gathered his officers to discuss what to do (Rutledge was no longer with Buford at this stage). There was no palatable option; outright surrender, a ditching of the wagons to increase the column's speed or a last stand using the wagons as makeshift fortifications all appeared to be either shameful actions or invitations to disaster. Buford decided to hope, pressing on with his march and trusting that he would meet up with other American forces before Tarleton reached him.

This was not necessarily a vain hope. Tarleton's command was slowly evaporating in the heat of the South Carolina countryside as men and mounts found it impossible to maintain the punishing pace set by their commander, but just two hours after Buford had been given the option of surrender, Tarleton's advanced guard met and captured Buford's five-man rearguard and the two forces began to form for battle. Tarleton placed 60 Legion dragoons, along with a near equal number of infantry, on his right flank. The infantry were to dismount, 'to gall the enemy's flank'. The 17th Light Dragoons and more Legion cavalry occupied the centre, while Tarleton commanded the left wing, with 30 'chosen horse' and the rest of the infantry, although he did not specify in his battle report if these men were dismounted as were those on the right flank. A small hill in the rear of the British line was earmarked for stragglers. They could gather there as they arrived and the hill was also the designated regrouping position should the assault fail.

Buford's dispositions for the battle have been widely criticized. He formed his Continentals up in a single line and made them hold their fire as the British approached. Many historians have remarked that he could have used his wagons as obstacles to impede the British cavalry and could also have made use of the two 6-pdr field pieces he had with him. Preventing his men from opening fire on the British earlier also prevented them from potentially disrupting the charge. The Virginians, showing remarkable courage, held their fire as ordered until the charging British troopers were a mere ten yards away. The ensuing volley had some effect, but nowhere near enough to stop the charge.

Buford's own battle report appears to lose credibility at this point of the battle, claiming that he was opposed by a force twice the size of his own. He mentioned the actions of the dismounted infantry on his left flank and stated

There is still confusion over whether Buford attempted a formal surrender at Waxhaws (and Tarleton may not have received the offer had it been made) but in the heat of battle the Virginia Continentals were completely routed by the British. (Anne S. K. Brown Military Collection)

that his men gave way under pressure, but retreated 50 yards and re-formed. At this point, with further resistance futile, Buford claims to have attempted to surrender. The circumstances of the attempted surrender are clouded in doubt. Many sources claim that Tarleton rejected the request and that his men indulged in a vicious killing spree, massacring the Americans, in many cases after they had thrown down their arms. The casualty list from the battle is undoubtedly one-sided in the extreme. The Americans lost 113 men killed, with 203 captured (150 of these were wounded), while British losses were just five dead and 14 wounded. Whether this was the result of a massacre (some sources claim that British troops prowled the battlefield for 15 minutes after fighting had ceased, bayoneting anyone who showed signs of life) is doubtful, and Buford's own account is coloured by the fact that he himself fled the battlefield.

Tarleton reported that his horse had been shot out from under him early in the encounter and had trapped him on the ground for a while, suggesting that at least some of his men thought he had been killed. Tarleton believed this might have enraged his men, which is tacit admission that their treatment of the Americans was unusually harsh. Buford's tactics must also have played their part in the heavy casualty list. Rather than setting up a defence in depth, or opening fire at greater range, the single line he presented was hit along its entire length by the British. Even assuming that 20 per cent of Tarleton's men took no part in the battle because of exhaustion, that would still have left him with nearly 140 mounted men. Being allowed to charge home with almost no interference (apart from the single, largely ineffective volley at extremely close range), those 140 men must have inflicted many of the casualties suffered by Buford's men in the initial moment of impact. After this, in the chaos of battle, any effort at a formal surrender would need to have been offered, recognized and accepted in an impossibly brief time span if the shattered Americans were not to be mown down by the rampant cavalry. Individual instances of soldiers being killed or injured while personally offering surrender must undoubtedly have existed, but it is impossible to know how widespread this was. The remorseless nature of Tarleton's approach to war, however, cannot be doubted. Having driven his men and horses up to and, in many cases, past their breaking point, and having covered 105 miles in 54 hours, he charged without a second thought and completely destroyed Buford's command. The last substantial Continental force in South Carolina had been eradicated.

The original Waxhaws monument, now difficult to read, marks the spot where as many as 80 of Buford's command are buried. Whatever the truth of the battle, 'Tarleton's Quarter', meaning no quarter at all, entered the American vocabulary after Waxhaws. (Photo by Stuart Morgan)

TARLETON'S QUARTER (PP. 52–53)

Banastre Tarleton's men (**1**) were already exhausted when they charged against the thin line of Virginia Continentals thrown over the road by Abraham Buford. Tarleton himself wondered why Buford had not created a more robust defensive position, perhaps using his wagons and cannon to form a makeshift redoubt. A position as strong as this, Tarleton suggested, might have dissuaded him from attacking at all.

Tarleton was also amazed that the Americans held their fire until the British were a mere 10 yards (**2**) from their line which 'prevented their [the Legion dragoons] falling into confusion on the charge'.

Tarleton has a hell-for-leather reputation, but his identification of a ridge of high ground as a potential rallying point should his charge fail to break the Americans shows that he was not completely reckless, and the Americans might have held their line had they not broken. Horses will not charge home against a dense and unbroken line of bayonets, and many an infantry square has held out against enemy cavalry.

Tarleton's own words are once more revealing in respect to this. Writing of the dragoons 'so effectually breaking the infantry', it seems likely that the American line lost cohesion on the approach of the British cavalry and a total rout ensued.

Three of the 3rd Virginia Detachment colours were captured at the battle and remained in the possession of the Tarleton family until 2006, when they were sold at auction, fetching the remarkable price of $5.056 million.

The anonymous buyer may well have been especially tempted by the main regimental colour (visible in the centre of the American line) which is believed to include the first depiction of 13 white stars on a blue background (**3**).

Tarleton already had a formidable reputation prior to Waxhaws, but he would subsequently be known as 'Ban the Butcher', or 'Bloody Ban', and he was a gift to patriot propagandists. He did, however, take as much care as possible of the wounded from both sides, calling for surgeons from Camden and Charlotte, although within the context of 18th-century medicine, this would have been small comfort.

CORNWALLIS TAKES COMMAND

According to the timetable of the British strategy, all appeared to be going to plan. Organized American forces had been eliminated from the colony and control was spreading into the back-country. It was at this point that Clinton made his final preparations to depart the scene, and his orders to Cornwallis had a familiar ring to them. The commander in the south was to view the safety of Charleston as his first priority, but Clinton pointed out, '... it is by no means my intention to prevent your acting offensively in case an opportunity should offer consistent with the security of this place, which is always to be regarded as a primary object'. Clinton had once railed under almost identical instructions from Howe, while in command at New York in 1777. The orders seemed framed as much to protect Clinton in the event of a disaster in the south as to give Cornwallis any real freedom to act.

Cornwallis would also have to deal with a shortage of weapons with which to supply the envisioned militia units. An explosion in the Charleston magazine, apparently caused when a loaded musket had been thrown to the ground and thus discharged, had taken the lives of more than 30 British soldiers and many civilians, as well as costing a great deal of powder and around 5,000 muskets. Only 2,000 muskets were safely stored in boxes, with around 1,600 or so recovered from the explosion in either an operational or repairable condition.

Cornwallis was already suspecting that Clinton was leaving him in a difficult situation. This impression could only have been strengthened by a series of proclamations made by Clinton before he left the south for good. On 1 June he called on the 'deluded subjects' of the colony to return to their former state of obedience and thus earn a full and free pardon for their 'treasonable offences'. Two days later, Clinton went further in a separate proclamation. This stated that a mere apology was not good enough – all citizens must now declare themselves willing to actually assist the British forces in restoring control over the colony, or be considered as enemies of the Crown. This remarkable proclamation effectively tore up the terms under which the Americans had surrendered at Charleston. The paroled militia must now choose either to offer its services to the British, or once more be considered to be in revolt. Simply staying out of the way and making its own peace with the British was no longer an option.

Having issued his incendiary proclamations, Clinton sailed for New York on 8 June, taking just ten days to retrace a journey that had consumed the best part of a month at the beginning of the year. Cornwallis seems to have had a sense of foreboding at this stage. He was worried that Clinton would make demands on his already meagre forces in the south in order to implement his planned operations in the Chesapeake – Clinton had in fact mused on

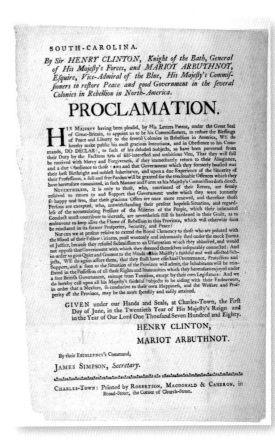

Clinton delivered three proclamations before exiting the stage in the south. Their impact is debated; Cornwallis quickly rejected some of the key elements of the proclamations, but they were a gift for patriot propaganda purposes. (Library of Congress)

The build-up of forces at Camden

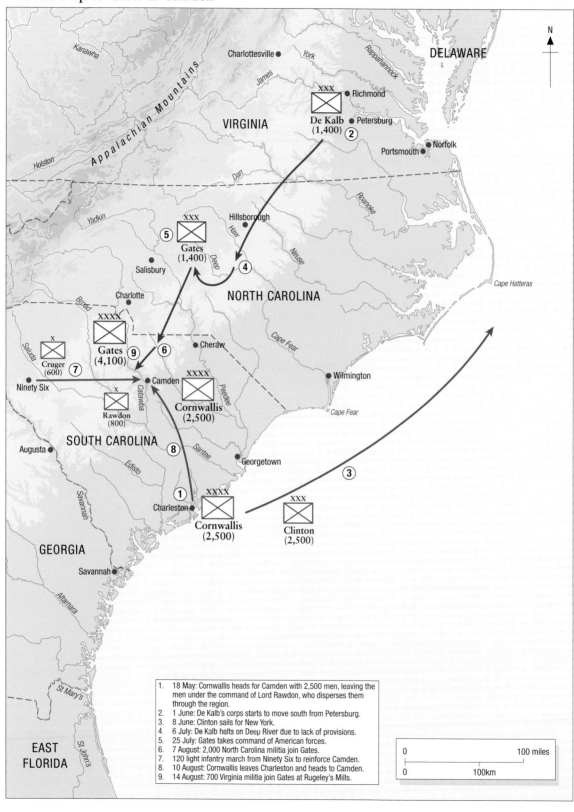

1. 18 May: Cornwallis heads for Camden with 2,500 men, leaving the men under the command of Lord Rawdon, who disperses them through the region.
2. 1 June: De Kalb's corps starts to move south from Petersburg.
3. 8 June: Clinton sails for New York.
4. 6 July: De Kalb halts on Deep River due to lack of provisions.
5. 25 July: Gates takes command of American forces.
6. 7 August: 2,000 North Carolina militia join Gates.
7. 120 light infantry march from Ninety Six to reinforce Camden.
8. 10 August: Cornwallis leaves Charleston and heads to Camden.
9. 14 August: 700 Virginia militia join Gates at Rugeley's Mills.

the possibility of Cornwallis heading for the Chesapeake with no fewer than 3,000 men, once North and South Carolina were returned to tranquillity (this out of a total force numbering a little less than 6,500). Clinton suggested that this might be accomplished by September or October, and Cornwallis must have thought this at best hopeful and at worst deluded. To Balfour on 11 June he remarked that 'every measure taken at Charlestown has counteracted me as much as possible', while on the 20th he noted that Clinton appeared to have taken all the wagons and horses in Charleston with him when he sailed for New York. Cornwallis also had reason to be dissatisfied with Clinton's choice for Commandant of Charleston. Paterson appeared overwhelmed by the position and Cornwallis was soon to replace him with Balfour.

Ferguson was another problem – the Inspector of Militia had drawn negative comments from Balfour and Cornwallis had insisted that he do nothing towards embodying militia units until he received detailed orders. The fact was that Ferguson had already received detailed orders, from Clinton, but the Scottish officer was cowed into passivity by Cornwallis's order; Balfour noted with satisfaction on 6 June that Ferguson had been 'perfectly quiet since he received your letter'. Cornwallis was right to be cautious about forming militia units. Drawing on a more conservative section of society, the loyalists needed to be carefully formed and were vulnerable to being scattered quickly by their more active patriot counterparts. In any event, the loyalists had already started to form their own units spontaneously. These 'associations' were viewed very favourably by Balfour, who noted that they knew much better than the British possibly could, who the trustworthy men of a region were. Balfour and Cornwallis agreed that these informal associations could be quickly transformed into more official militia units when the time was right. Timing, in fact, was very much a critical issue. A premature rising of loyalist militia in early 1776 had been disastrous, with a large body of Scots loyalists scattered at Moore's Creek Bridge, in North Carolina. Cornwallis was determined to prevent the same thing from happening again and urged the North Carolina loyalists to be patient and

During the British occupation of Camden extensive defensive works were built, but they also made use of existing structures. The foundations of the powder magazine (built in 1777 and originally having 48in. brick walls) can still be seen… (Photo by Stuart Morgan)

… as can the earthworks that were constructed around the magazine. Such a structure would not only protect the magazine, it would also help to contain any explosion within the magazine itself. The building was destroyed during the battle of Hobkirk's Hill in 1781. (Photo by Stuart Morgan)

await the arrival of British troops before rising up. The lack of provisions in the province (Cornwallis described the North Carolina back-country as being in a state close to famine) meant that British intervention could not be expected until after the harvest had been gathered.

Cornwallis's own thoughts on the formation of militia units were laid out in his 'Draft plan for dealing with the disaffected and the militia', while at Camden on 4 June. This largely conformed to Clinton's own proposal as submitted to Ferguson. The loyalists were to be divided into two groups, those thought able to embark on offensive operations away from home and those expected to do nothing more than respond to local crises. Cornwallis also detailed what was to be done about the patriot militia. Field officers and those who had held official public posts (such as governor or members of the council) were to be imprisoned on the various islands off the coast of Charleston (James, John's, Edisto, St Helena and Port Royal were all mentioned). Joining these would be any who had been 'particularly obnoxious to friends of Government'. 'Violent persecutors' would likewise be imprisoned, while the less active patriots would be allowed to remain in their homes on parole, although they would be disarmed. This last proviso clashed clearly with Clinton's inflammatory proclamation of 3 June and when Cornwallis received word of this, he quickly wrote to Paterson at Charleston, expressing his disagreement with Clinton's actions.

A selection of field guns used in the defence of Camden. A British 6-pdr lies in the centre, with two French four-pounders flanking it. In the background a replica gun carriage can be seen. (Photo by Stuart Morgan)

'It is with great concern,' he wrote on 10 June, 'that I find the Commander in Chief adopted the idea of granting indiscriminate protections, by which means some of the most violent rebels and persecutors of the whole province are declared faithful subjects and are promised to be protected in their persons and properties… All persons who have got these protections, and who cannot in the opinion of the commanding officers of each district be safely received into the [loyalist] militia, must be obliged to give up their protections, and their paroles must be taken as prisoners of war… I should wish it to be publicly known that no more protections will be granted and that those already given will be recalled unless the conduct and characters of the possessors entitle them to be trusted to bear arms in the militia or provincial corps.'

The rapidity with which he moved to dismantle the structure set up by the 3 June proclamation inevitably calls into question the effect the proclamation had. It has long been considered a disastrous blunder that forced patriots to take up arms once more, but clearly Cornwallis was willing that they should be allowed to return to their position as paroled prisoners of war. The reality is not quite so simple, however, as patriot propagandists were always able to make better use of opportunities such as this and the damage done by Clinton could not be quickly undone. The Commander-in-Chief would later try to absolve himself of responsibility for the negative effects of his proclamation, claiming that Cornwallis had the authority to implement it as he saw fit, but this did not take into account the psychological effect. Cornwallis confided in Balfour once more on the matter, saying he had been startled by the impact it had made on the population. Rawdon also commented on 'that unfortunate proclamation of 3 June'.

The men left actually to run the war in the south were clearly unhappy with the decisions made by Clinton before he left for New York, but with the Commander-in-Chief out of the way, perhaps they could still rescue the situation. As far as Clinton was concerned, he was destined for a frustrating few months in New York in the company of Arbuthnot. The French force (6,000 men and seven ships of the line) reached Rhode Island in early July and, despite endless wrangling over potential plans to dislodge them, Clinton and Arbuthnot eventually did precisely nothing. The French would find their foothold at Rhode Island very useful the next year, when they were able to combine with other French and American units at Yorktown.

On 21 June Cornwallis left Camden to return to Charleston. Arriving on 25 June he quickly decided that Paterson would need to be replaced, calling Balfour to Charleston on the pretext that Paterson had fallen ill. Cornwallis was successfully reshaping the infrastructure of British control of the colony, but he was finding it harder to influence events outside his direct control and the situation was already beginning to deteriorate when Paterson left Charleston, on 18 July. The situation in North Carolina had taken a decided turn for the worse when loyalist militia repeated the error of four years previously and rose up prematurely. From the middle of June a large body of loyalists had been gathering at Ramsour's Mill under Colonel John Moore.

The fleur-de-lis on one of the French 4-pdrs betrays its heritage. The two French cannon on display at Camden were captured at Louisburg in 1758. They were spiked and abandoned by the British when they evacuated Camden. (Photo by Stuart Morgan)

Originally built around 1777 (although still unfinished when the British arrived), the mansion of Joseph Kershaw was used as headquarters by Rawdon and Cornwallis during the occupation of Camden. It was burned down in the Civil War and reconstructed between 1974 and 1977. (Photo by Stuart Morgan)

Finally numbering more than 1,300 men, they were nevertheless a weak and disorganized force (as many as a quarter of the men had no weapons at all) and were scattered by a smaller patriot force on 20 June in a chaotic battle. Cornwallis was furious at this clear breach of his instructions and Rawdon immediately saw the dangers inherent in such a setback, commenting that 'this advantage on the part of the rebels may shake the fidelity of our new-formed militia on the borders unless the troops are present to awe them to their duty'. Further complications were added when another North Carolina uprising saw 1,500 militia gather around Colonel Samuel Bryan, the bulk of whom quickly marched into South Carolina to present the British with a logistical headache and hundreds of new mouths to feed. Within weeks Cornwallis was faced with a dilemma. He could either move into North Carolina sooner than he had planned, or leave the loyalists in that colony to the tender mercies of the patriots.

The situation was also worsening in South Carolina. Balfour (before being called to Charleston) reported that the rebels were stirring things up nicely in the vicinity of Ninety Six and had largely cowed the loyalist element. On 12 July, a force including Legion cavalry and commanded by Captain Christian Huck was completely routed (with the death of Huck and a further 34 men) at Williamson's Plantation. On 15 July a small force of loyalist militia had attacked what it believed to be a party of 25 Georgia militia near present-day Spartanburg, only to have the tables turned on them when no fewer than 400 rebels counterattacked. Sumter was threatening Rawdon's positions around Camden with an estimated 1,500 men, a situation that highlighted clearly the problem faced by the British. Rawdon had no doubts that he could advance upon Sumter's force and drive them away, but without leaving regular troops to guard the region, Sumter would simply return when Rawdon himself moved back to Camden. It was simply impossible to secure a large region without dispersing forces in dangerously small parcels of men. This might be possible when small bands of militia were the only opposition, but it was inviting disaster if a large organized enemy force entered a region, which is exactly what happened next.

Actions in the South prior to Camden, 1780

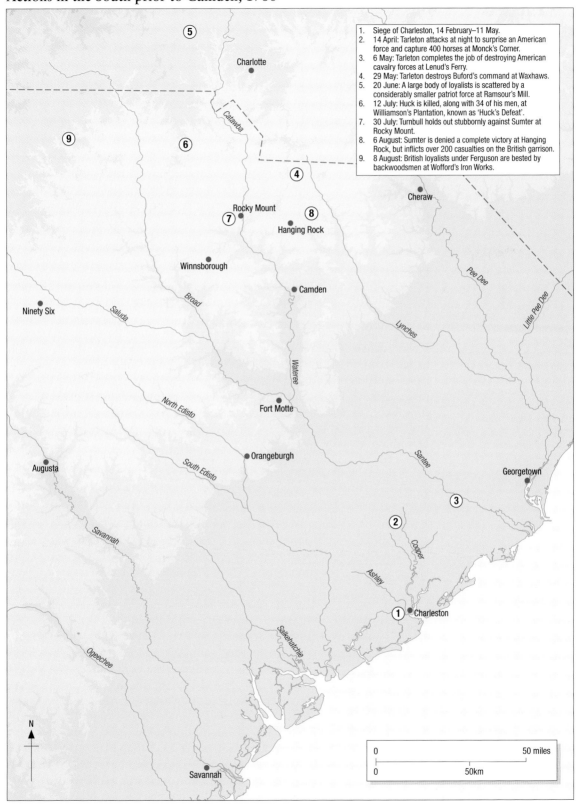

1. Siege of Charleston, 14 February–11 May.
2. 14 April: Tarleton attacks at night to surprise an American force and capture 400 horses at Monck's Corner.
3. 6 May: Tarleton completes the job of destroying American cavalry forces at Lenud's Ferry.
4. 29 May: Tarleton destroys Buford's command at Waxhaws.
5. 20 June: A large body of loyalists is scattered by a considerably smaller patriot force at Ramsour's Mill.
6. 12 July: Huck is killed, along with 34 of his men, at Williamson's Plantation, known as 'Huck's Defeat'.
7. 30 July: Turnbull holds out stubbornly against Sumter at Rocky Mount.
8. 6 August: Sumter is denied a complete victory at Hanging Rock, but inflicts over 200 casualties on the British garrison.
9. 8 August: British loyalists under Ferguson are bested by backwoodsmen at Wofford's Iron Works.

Charlotte

Catawba

Cheraw

Rocky Mount
Hanging Rock

Winnsborough

Pee Dee

Camden

Broad

Ninety Six

Saluda

Lynches

Little Pee Dee

Wateree

North Edisto

Fort Motte

Orangeburgh

South Edisto

Santee

Augusta

Georgetown

Savannah

Cooper

Ashley

Charleston

Salkehatchie

Ogeechee

N

0 ————————————— 50 miles
0 ————————————— 50km

Savannah

THE FORMATION OF THE 'GRAND ARMY'

Rumours of an American army marching down from the south had been circulating since May. Recognizing the dire situation in South Carolina, a substantial force of Continentals under de Kalb had been dispatched by Washington on 16 April. De Kalb was on the move with two Maryland brigades composed of seven Maryland regiments and a single regiment from Delaware, around 1,400 men who could claim to be among the finest in the entire Continental Army. Initially the force was divided, with supply and ammunition wagons proceeding overland along with the artillery, while the troops embarked at the Head of Elk on 3 May. The two sections of the army met up once more at Petersburg and, after awaiting provision of wagons from Virginia, de Kalb divided his force into three brigades, the first two of which set off for the south on 1 and 6 June respectively. At this point de Kalb learned that Charleston had fallen and was uncertain of how to proceed, before deciding that the presence of an army in the south could still hinder British plans. By 20 June, de Kalb's army was in North Carolina, but by 6 July they were forced to halt at a point on Deep River when lack of provisions became desperate. Foraging parties were sent out but had to compete with the North Carolina militia, who had effectively picked the area clean.

At this point the first effort was made to combine the Continentals with the substantial militia operating under General Richard Caswell, but Caswell ignored de Kalb's request to join with his men. Further requests would also be ignored and the army would not properly take shape until 7 August, by which time command had passed to Gates. The hero of Saratoga took over from de Kalb on 24 July and dubbed his command the 'Grand Army'. Although in a dishevelled state and suffering terribly from hunger, fatigue and the attentions of swarms of biting insects, the army marked the transfer of command with as much pomp and circumstance as it could muster, including a 13-gun salute. The long-awaited addition of around 2,000 North Carolina militia certainly gave Gates a sizeable force, one that Rawdon tracked with growing concern as it neared Camden.

Cornwallis may well have been relieved at the approach of a sizeable army. Charleston was, in his words, 'in the most confused state' by the middle of July and the prospect of a straight fight against a conventional enemy must have appealed. This was the sort of work Cornwallis understood and he had confidence rooted in extensive experience. By 15 July he was writing to Rawdon that it was 'absolutely necessary to act offensively very soon to save our friends in North Carolina and to preserve the confidence, in which is included the friendship, of the South Carolinians'. Cornwallis declared, with apparent relief, that he would soon leave Charleston once more and join Rawdon at Camden with the aim of launching an offensive into North Carolina. It was earlier than planned and had in large part been forced upon him, but it was preferable to sitting on his heels in Charleston as the entire British position in the south crumbled around him.

French forces were able to land unopposed at Rhode Island when Royal Navy ships lost contact with the French fleet. Clinton and Arbuthnot then failed to agree on a plan of attack to remove them and they remained untroubled until called upon to move on Yorktown the following year. (Library of Congress)

Rawdon had dispersed his men around Camden, taking up positions at Hanging Rock, Black Creek, Rocky Mount and Cheraws Hill. There had been two main reasons for this. Firstly, it allowed him to extend British control over a wider area and secondly it got as many of his men as possible out of Camden, which had turned out to be a particularly unhealthy place (Rawdon himself had suffered a bout of debilitating fever, which he called 'ague'). British troops were once more massing at Camden, however, as the approach of Gates made it necessary to concentrate forces. The post of Cheraws Hill had also been abandoned when the garrisoning force, the 71st Regiment, had suffered a serious outbreak of fever. As many as 90 stricken men had been evacuated by boat, aiming for Georgetown, but had been captured when local loyalist militia had turned coat and joined the rebels. 'The whole country,' Rawdon wrote, 'is in confusion and uproar.'

If the British could have known the difficulties being experienced by Gates, however, they might have felt a little better. The American army was in a greatly weakened state as it approached the South Carolina border. After taking over command of the army, Gates had opted for a direct march towards Camden through an exhausted and generally hostile country. A lengthier march could have taken the army through territory better able to support his army and populated by more revolutionary elements, and this option had been pressed upon him by various officers, including de Kalb. Gates was later defended by an aide-de-camp, Major Thomas Pinckney. Writing more than 40 years after the event, he claimed that Gates had taken the direct route in order to link up as quickly as possible with Caswell's North Carolina militia, who had ignored repeated orders to join the Grand

'Huck's Defeat', one of a string of actions during the upswell of resistance to their presence in the south. Banastre Tarleton was incensed that a number of his Legion cavalrymen had been lent to William Huck prior to this engagement. (Painting by Don Troiani)

Army and were in danger of being picked off by Rawdon if a swift juncture was not made. Whatever the real reason for Gates' decision, his men had been marched to the point of exhaustion by the time they reached Caswell. Gates apparently had no concerns about the state of his army, however. After lining up with Caswell, the march continued and a Virginia militiaman would later complain that they had been forced to march 'almost night and day and kept on half allowance of flour for eight or 10 days before the battle'.

The apparent urgency of the Americans' march is curious. Merely by his presence, Gates was interfering greatly with British plans. The need to concentrate forces meant that the support of regulars was withdrawn from a large area, allowing patriot elements to re-establish control. Gates' army, with its strong core of Continental regiments, could also act as a magnet for smaller units of militia, and offered them a place of refuge to fall back on if pressed by the British. In short, there was no hurry and Gates may well have gone a long way to eroding British control in South Carolina simply by keeping his army intact. Washington had achieved much the same thing (largely by accident, it must be admitted, as his instinct was to be aggressive) when he had kept the kernel of his army intact after the battering administered by Howe during the 1776 campaign. The British were clearly struggling with the flare-up of partisan activity and the battle to win hearts and minds, nor were they as adept at this form of warfare as their patriot opposition. By advancing quickly, Gates was allowing the British to change the game to one much more to their liking; they understood battle, and they were good at it.

ROCKY MOUNT AND HANGING ROCK

Rawdon had avoided calling all his men into Camden, although he was aware that he would eventually have no choice but to do just that. For now

Colonel George Turnbull's defence of Rocky Mount was brave and determined, but also owed a debt of gratitude to a fortuitous downpour of rain. (Author's collection)

he wanted to withdraw slowly, to impede Gates' progress and give time for reinforcements to reach Camden. Those reinforcements were pathetically small in number (four depleted companies of light infantry from Ninety Six, numbering around 120 men, and cavalry under Tarleton on its way from Charleston), but could yet make all the difference if it came to a battle. Rawdon's advanced posts at Rocky Mount and Hanging Rock therefore became targets for the advancing Americans. It was Sumter's large band of militia that set its sights on the two exposed positions.

Sumter was experiencing all the vagaries of commanding militia. His men quickly grew tired of inactivity and it was only by keeping them in action that he could hope to preserve his force. The 300-man garrison at Rocky Mount (150 militia and 150 provincials of the New York Volunteers, commanded by Lieutenant-Colonel George Turnbull) made a tempting target and Sumter led around 500 of his militia against them on 30 July. The position at Rocky Mount was strong, with three log cabins surrounded by a ditch and abatis. The cabins had been strengthened to resist rifle fire and loopholes had been cut in the walls. Sumter attempted three charges on the cabins and even managed to set one of the cabins on fire but, just as it appeared the British might be forced to surrender, an untimely downpour extinguished the flames. Casualties were light (about 12 killed or wounded on each side) in a skirmish that lasted around eight hours, but Sumter was forced eventually to abandon the assault. Rawdon had been visiting the garrison at Hanging Rock at the time and was frustrated when a party of loyalists driven away before the main assault on Rocky Mount fled to Camden rather than Hanging Rock. He believed he could have cut off Sumter's retreat if alerted in time, turning an inconclusive skirmish into a major British victory.

Rawdon received reports of the rebels approaching Rocky Mount again on 1 August and sent substantial reinforcements. Deterred from attacking on account of the increased garrison, but recognizing the need to keep his restless militia engaged, Sumter switched his attention to the post at Hanging Rock. On 6 August he initiated a serious engagement that cost the lives of 20 patriots and 25 loyalists and provincials (wounded numbered 40 and 175 respectively, and 73 of the British forces were also captured).

Sumter had been forced to break off his attack, but he had come close to a major victory. Had the British not shuttled back the reinforcements sent from Hanging Rock to Rocky Mount on 1 August, they would almost

The huge boulder that gave the British position at Hanging Rock its name. The battle of 6 August was actually fought some distance away. (Photo by Stuart Morgan)

certainly have been defeated. As it was, Sumter ran into a substantial garrison comprising men of the Prince of Wales American Regiment, a hundred men of the North Carolina Regiment, a detachment of British Legion infantry and two units of loyalist militia (Bryan's North Carolina Volunteers and Colonel Henry Rugeley's Camden District Militia) for a total strength of around 1,300. Sumter himself commanded around 600 men. In a hard-fought encounter lasting several hours (Sumter reported many men passing out from heat exhaustion), the battle ebbed and flowed. The Americans had gained an early advantage when Bryan's loyalist militia broke and fled back to the main British camp. The commanding officer of the British forces, Major John Carden from the Prince of Wales Regiment, organized a counter-attack that was beaten back and then appears to have lost his nerve, handing over command to Captain Rousselet of the Legion infantry. Carden nevertheless helped with the organization of a hollow square, which kept Sumter's men at bay (the Americans were hampered by the fact that several hundred of them were pillaging British supplies in the camp rather than pursuing a victory that had seemed to be theirs for the taking). Frustrated, Sumter was eventually forced to withdraw.

One of a string of fortifications surrounding Camden, the Southeast Redoubt was built near the Kershaw house and comprised a moat, an open parapet and a palisade wall. The reconstructed redoubt is based on an American army map of 1781. (Photo by Stuart Morgan)

When Rawdon, at a position on Lynches Creek, first heard of the assault, he believed the Americans had captured the entire garrison at Hanging Rock. Fearing that he might be caught between Sumter and Gates, he had his force of 1,100 men on the march within half an hour, but the following morning he learned that Sumter had been repulsed and instead took up a new position on the west fork of Little Lynches Creek. Here Rawdon waited with the 23rd, the 33rd and the depleted 71st, along with the Volunteers of Ireland, a body of militia and 40 Legion dragoons. The strength of his command, and the fact that Gates would have been forced to advance over an exposed river crossing to get at him, persuaded the American general that a flanking march would be more prudent and he wheeled his army away towards Rugeley's Mills, around 13 miles from Camden. A unit of Legion infantry fell back from Rugeley's Mills as Gates approached and the stage was set for the battle of Camden. Rawdon had delayed Gates as long as he could. He reported to Cornwallis that the American army was reckoned to be 5,000 strong, but that he personally doubted it could be any more than 3,500 (a perceptive assessment, as it turned out), and concentrated his forces about one mile outside of Camden. Cornwallis was by now on his way, but Rawdon was not sure he would arrive in time. 'Gates may attack me tomorrow morning,' he wrote on 11 August. 'If he does, I think he will find us in better spirits than he expects.'

THE BATTLE OF CAMDEN

Exactly what Gates was hoping to achieve on the night of 15–16 August is not clear. He has been criticized for advancing to attack Camden with a force so heavily dependent upon untested militia, but the defence offered by some (that he was only moving to a stronger position and had no intention of actually attacking the British) deserves serious consideration. Some of the strongest criticism of Gates came from Colonel Otho Holland Williams of the Marylanders, acting as the Deputy Adjutant General of the army, but conflicting evidence was offered by other officers close to Gates and presumably familiar with his thinking.

On 14 August Gates was joined by 700 Virginia militia under Brigadier-General Edward Stevens and he decided to move. What the move was intended to achieve is open to debate. Several witnesses claim that the intention was to attack the British at Camden, but it is not clear how many men Gates believed were with Rawdon. It is often assumed that Cornwallis brought reinforcements with him from Charleston and that this inflated the size of the army facing Gates, but apart from his personal escort Cornwallis brought no new troops. There were something like 2,500 men at Camden, with several hundred unfit for duty following the outbreaks of fever. This might have appeared a tempting target for Gates, who apparently believed his own force now numbered around 7,000.

Even so, there is compelling evidence that Gates was intending only to take up a threatening position closer to Camden when he ordered a march towards that post on the night of 15 August. Colonel John Christian Serf, a European engineer with Gates, reconnoitred the route to Camden and personally recommended a spot about halfway between Camden and Rugeley's Mills. At this point the Americans would be able to take up a commanding position overlooking Saunders Creek, which was supposedly impassable for seven miles both upstream and downstream of the crossing Gates would be defending. The British would need either to risk a potentially costly frontal assault or embark on a lengthy outflanking march that would leave Camden exposed, if they wanted to force him to move. At a council of his officers Gates proposed the march, although some would complain that his manner had deterred any questioning of the plan.

Williams, alarmed that Gates had such an inflated view of his own numbers, took a hasty strength report from each American unit and came up with a figure of just 3,052 rank and file fit for duty. Gates appeared surprised at this news, but commented that it was 'enough for our purpose'. If the purpose had been simply to occupy an advantageous piece of ground, then Gates may have been justified in his opinion. If his purpose was to attack the British at Camden, then his army was worryingly small, with the bulk of it being militia. Worse than that, the militia in Gates' army was from North Carolina or Virginia and militia units were notorious for being unsteady when far from home. Gates had actually weakened his army prior to setting off on his night march. Around 300 North Carolina militia and 100 precious Maryland Continentals, along with two 3-pdrs, had been detached to join Sumter, who offered to threaten Camden's lines of communication, blocking both supplies and reinforcements from reaching the

Some of the most damning criticism of Horatio Gates' command during the battle of Camden came from Colonel Otho H. Williams. The Marylander, filling the role of Deputy Adjutant General at the time, had little positive to say about his commanding officer. (Library of Congress)

The Great Wagon Road, along which British and American armies marched during the night of 15–16 August, can still be seen today, although it is now little more than a faint depression through the pine trees. (Photo by Stuart Morgan)

town. As the final element of preparation, Gates famously gave his men a meal involving a large helping of molasses, which, due to its effect on their digestive systems, caused great inconvenience to them throughout the night.

They set out at 10.00pm on 15 August. At about the same time, Cornwallis left Camden. There is no ambiguity about his intentions. Intelligence suggested that Gates was poorly posted at Rugeley's Mills and Cornwallis intended to attack him. In one of the great coincidences of the war, the two armies were marching towards each other on the same road, at the same time, each unaware that its enemy was also advancing.

Cornwallis had arrived at Camden on the 13th. His planned invasion of North Carolina had now been superseded by the presence of Gates, and Cornwallis, believing the American army to be considerably larger than it actually was, knew he had a fight on his hands. He first ordered the best horses in the British garrison to be given up for the use of Tarleton's cavalry and he then augmented his ranks with the most able of the invalids. Every man would be crucial. On the 15th he dispatched Tarleton on a mission to capture rebel soldiers and extract intelligence from them. Three patriot militiamen subsequently told how they had been left at Lynches Creek to recover from illness and had been hurrying to catch up with Gates when they were caught. According to the three men, Gates' intention was to attack the British at Camden, but how much they could have known of Gates' actual plan is obviously questionable.

Cornwallis needed no further encouragement and a rumour swept through the British ranks that Gates had boasted he would eat his dinner in Camden or in hell the following evening. Though obviously untrue, it may have served to fire the British soldiers with enthusiasm and if John Robert Shaw of the 33rd Regiment was accurate in recording an address made by Cornwallis prior to their departure, they must have been wound up to a state of great excitement as they left. According to Shaw, Cornwallis delivered a rousing speech: 'Now, my brave soldiers, now an opportunity is offered for displaying your valour, and sustaining the glory of the British arms. All you who are willing to face your enemies, all you who are ambitious of military fame stand forward, for there are eight or ten to one coming against. Let the man who cannot bear the smell of gunpowder stand back, and all you who are determined to conquer or die turn out.'

The British marched with Lieutenant-Colonel James Webster in the van with 20 Legion cavalry, 20 mounted infantry and the four companies of light infantry. Next came the 23rd and 33rd regiments, then Rawdon with the Volunteers of Ireland, the Legion infantry, Hamilton's corps and Bryan's

North Carolina troops. The two battalions of the 71st Regiment followed, with the rest of the Legion cavalry as a rearguard. Six pieces of artillery marched with the army. The British, numbering something less than 2,000 men, crossed Saunders Creek around midnight and needed to pause for a while to regain order (ironically, this is probably the point towards which Gates was marching). The moon was almost full and behind the British as they marched. Though low in the sky, it provided enough illumination for the marching men.

The Americans were marching in the opposite direction with the horses of Lieutenant-Colonel Charles Tuffin Armand's Legion of Horse and Foot in the van, flanked on the right by 50 light infantry and 150 Virginia militia and on the left by 200 North Carolina militia, each about 200 yards out from the road. The light infantry of Armand's Legion followed, with the 1st and 2nd Maryland brigades next, then the North Carolina and Virginia militia, with a rearguard made up of volunteer cavalry. Ammunition and baggage wagons brought up the rear. The two armies edged ever closer to each other until, around 2.30am, the advanced units met. The moon was by now higher in the sky and North Carolina militiaman Guildford Dudley would later recall that it 'shone beautifully … consequently, we could see to fight in the open piney wood plains … as well in the night as in the day'. A sharp engagement broke out. Believing at first that this was merely a rebel patrol, the British resumed their march, only to run into the whole American army. Both sides deployed for action, the light infantry, 23rd and 33rd regiments lining up across the road on the British side and engaging in a 15-minute firefight with the American vanguard, although some of them (notably the Virginia militia) had fled. As if realizing that the time for a full-scale battle had not yet arrived, firing slowed and then ceased at the same time on both sides.

Mordecai Gist commanded the 2nd Maryland Brigade during the battle of Camden, forming the right wing of the main American line. The Marylanders and Delaware soldiers of his brigade performed heroically against superior numbers. (Library of Congress)

The battlefield at Camden today. Longleaf pine have been replanted to restore the site to its 18th-century condition, but the wiregrass that would have covered the ground on 16 August 1780 is absent. (Photo by Stuart Morgan)

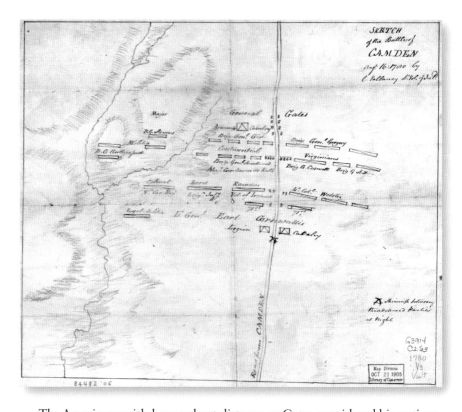

A sketch of the battle of Camden, produced by Charles Vallancey (an officer of the Volunteers of Ireland and therefore, presumably, an eyewitness to the battle). His arrangement of American troops, however, does not match most accounts of the battle. (Library of Congress)

William Smallwood commanded the 1st Maryland Brigade at the battle of Camden. Originally positioned as a reserve, they were called into the line almost immediately after Gates ordered his left wing to advance upon the British. (Library of Congress)

The Americans withdrew a short distance as Gates considered his options. Williams claimed the American commander could not hide his astonishment at meeting the British army, but at another council of his officers the decision was taken to stand and fight. Gates apparently asked his officers for options, only to be met by silence until Stevens said: 'Gentlemen, is it not too late now to do anything but fight?' De Kalb was apparently in favour of a withdrawal. That would have been difficult, although Cornwallis chose to hold his ground (Rawdon informed him that it was a good place to make the best use of his small numbers) and Gates would have had one or two precious hours in which to extricate his men.

At sunrise the next day, Cornwallis advanced his men around three-quarters of a mile to the new American position. Gates has been criticized for his deployment on the day of battle, but both generals put their best troops on their right. The difference was that Cornwallis could count on steady provincials such as the Volunteers of Ireland to hold his left wing, while Gates chanced everything on his inexperienced militia. The 400 men of the 1st Maryland Brigade were held in reserve and may have made a telling difference if they had been deployed along the Americans' main line.

It was a humid and still morning. The battlefield was dotted with mature longleaf pine trees, bare to a height of around 40ft, with wiregrass growing to a height of 2–3ft on the ground and underbrush sparse. Visibility was therefore good and manoeuvring easy, while marshy ground to each side prevented either force from outflanking the other. Gates had a few small advantages. He was on slightly rising ground and Cornwallis would have a creek behind him, which would cause problems if he was forced to retreat. The

The meeting of the armies on 16 August

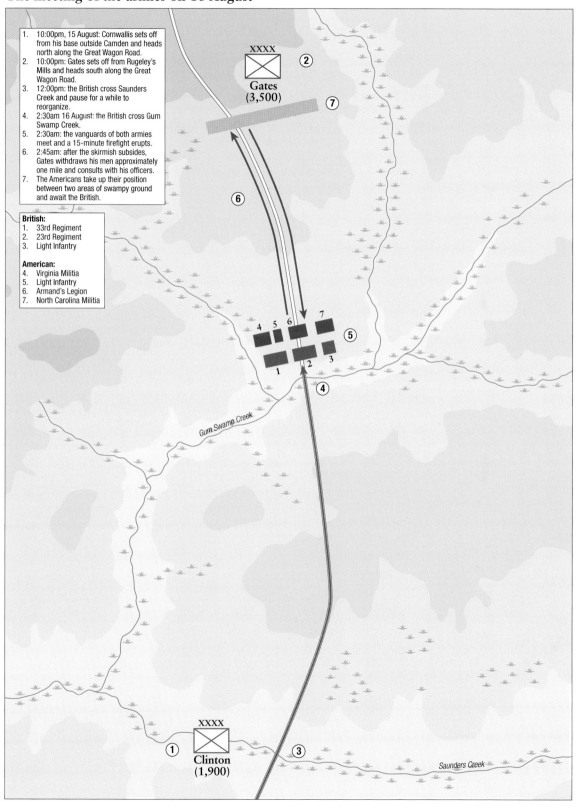

1. 10:00pm, 15 August: Cornwallis sets off from his base outside Camden and heads north along the Great Wagon Road.
2. 10:00pm: Gates sets off from Rugeley's Mills and heads south along the Great Wagon Road.
3. 12:00pm: the British cross Saunders Creek and pause for a while to reorganize.
4. 2:30am 16 August: the British cross Gum Swamp Creek.
5. 2:30am: the vanguards of both armies meet and a 15-minute firefight erupts.
6. 2:45am: after the skirmish subsides, Gates withdraws his men approximately one mile and consults with his officers.
7. The Americans take up their position between two areas of swampy ground and await the British.

British:
1. 33rd Regiment
2. 23rd Regiment
3. Light Infantry

American:
4. Virginia Militia
5. Light Infantry
6. Armand's Legion
7. North Carolina Militia

XXXX
Gates
(3,500)

Gum Swamp Creek

XXXX
Clinton
(1,900)

Saunders Creek

Americans formed with the 2nd Maryland Brigade on their right alongside the Delaware Regiment, commanded by Brigadier-General Mordecai Gist. Three brigades of North Carolina militia held the centre, while the 700 Virginia militia were next in line. Around 400 light infantry anchored the extreme left, with Armand's 100 mounted troopers behind them. The 1st Maryland Brigade (under Major-General William Smallwood) formed up 200 yards behind the main line. The few American guns were arranged with three straddling the road and two between the Marylanders and the Delaware Regiment. The remainder of the guns were with the Maryland reserve.

The battle opened when Cornwallis's men arrived, still in column, on the field. Gates had just delivered a few words of encouragement to his men when the three-gun battery across the road, commanded by Captain Anthony Singleton, opened fire with great effect. No solid shot has been recovered from the battlefield, and it would have been a poor choice in a wooded area and with the opposing armies so close to each other. It appears, therefore, that artillery on both sides used case shot exclusively. For a 6-pdr gun (Singleton's battery consisted of brass 6-pdrs), a case shot would contain around 56 cast iron balls, each weighing 1½ ounces. These deadly projectiles caught the British troops deploying from column into line and the 33rd Regiment bore the brunt. Major Thomas Pinckney, who was captured during the battle, claimed that an officer of the 33rd admitted that 60 men of his regiment had been killed or wounded by the first American fire. This seems excessive, but the 33rd certainly suffered badly in the battle, with 100 out of 298 killed, wounded or missing.

Williams saw another chance to disrupt the British as they deployed from column to line and urged Gates to order an advance from the left. This might have made tactical sense, but it was asking an awful lot of militia to advance against British regulars. Still, Gates agreed and Williams raced off to inform Stevens and the Virginia militia. Williams, in his highly critical report of the

This depiction of the battle of Camden does little to capture the true nature of what was a ferocious, albeit brief struggle (it also fails to recognize that the battle was fought in a pine forest). (Author's collection)

battle, claimed that this was the last order he received from Gates on the day and some historians have interpreted this as meaning it was the last order Gates made to anyone. It was not, as he immediately called on the Maryland reserve brigade to advance and fill the gap that would be left by Stevens' men, as well as asking de Kalb to advance with the 2nd Maryland Brigade to support Stevens. Williams, meanwhile, picked 50 or 60 men to advance as skirmishers in front of the main body of Virginia troops, aiming to draw an early fire from the British. The confusion of the moment, and the fact that these were untrained militia, is borne out by the British reaction. Observing the movement in the American ranks, Tarleton reported that it was interpreted as merely an attempt to rearrange their line. As such, it offered a chance for the British to attack, and Cornwallis took it.

By now the British were in line, with a similar deployment to the Americans. The right flank was held by (in order from right to left) four light infantry companies, the 23rd Regiment and the 33rd. This brigade, under Webster, deployed to the right of the road. To the left was Rawdon's brigade, comprising the Volunteers of Ireland, the British Legion infantry and 267 North Carolina loyalists. The two battalions of the 71st Regiment, along with another 300 or so loyalist militia, formed the reserve, while Tarleton's cavalry, still in column, waited its chance to exploit an opening in the enemy formation. Two 6-pdrs and two 3-pdrs were placed on the road to the right of the Volunteers of Ireland, while each battalion of the 71st had a 6-pdr.

The Maryland and Delaware troops of the 2nd Maryland Brigade took the fight to the forces under Lord Rawdon on the British left. Several bayonet charges were made before superior British numbers proved irresistible. (Library of Congress)

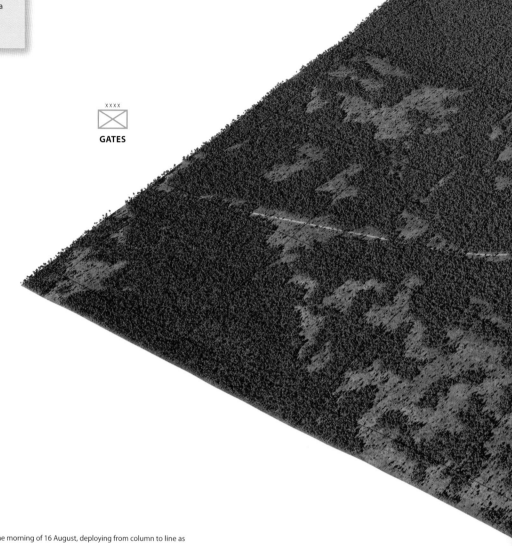

AMERICAN UNITS
A. 2nd Maryland Brigade
B. 1st Maryland Brigade
C. North Carolina militia
D. Virginia militia
E. Light infantry
F. Armand's Legion

xxxx
GATES

▼ EVENTS

1. The British advance on the morning of 16 August, deploying from column to line as the Americans wait.

2. Gates orders the Virginia militia to advance on the British.

3. Immediately afterwards, Gates orders the 1st Maryland Brigade to move up from its position in reserve to fill the gap left by the advancing Virginians.

4. The British, seeing movement in the American line, interpret it as an attempt at reorganization and a general advance is ordered by Cornwallis.

5. The 33rd Regiment takes the brunt of an opening artillery barrage as it advances.

6. Gates orders the 2nd Maryland Brigade forward to support the advance of the Virginians.

7. The Virginia militia break almost immediately as the British begin their advance and the panic quickly spreads to the rest of the militia in the American line. Soon only the two Maryland brigades and a small number of North Carolina militia remain as the bulk of Gates' army scatters in all directions.

THE BATTLE OF CAMDEN: FIRST PHASE

16 August 1780. Following a skirmish the previous night, British and American forces engaged in longleaf pine woodland on the road to Camden, flanked by swampland.

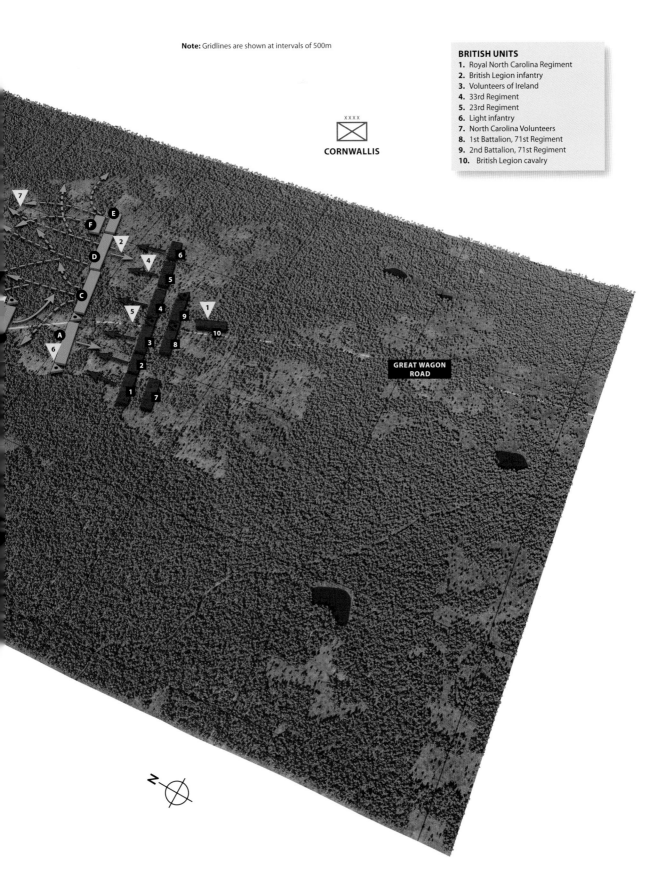

x x x x

CORNWALLIS

BRITISH UNITS
1. Royal North Carolina Regiment
2. British Legion infantry
3. Volunteers of Ireland
4. 33rd Regiment
5. 23rd Regiment
6. Light infantry
7. North Carolina Volunteers
8. 1st Battalion, 71st Regiment
9. 2nd Battalion, 71st Regiment
10. British Legion cavalry

GREAT WAGON
ROAD

Seeing the Americans in apparent confusion, Cornwallis personally ordered Webster to lead the right wing forward and sent an aide to give the same order to Rawdon on the left – both armies now advanced towards each other, but only for a few moments. The British regulars under Webster advanced quickly, cheering loudly, and the Virginia militia broke. Events during a battle are often clouded with uncertainty, but all sources confirm the rout of the Virginia militia and it was a critical moment. It happened so quickly that there had been no time for the Maryland reserve brigade to take its place in the line and the entire American position quickly unravelled (Tarleton believed that the militia had become 'somewhat deranged' by Gates' attempt at reorganization). The panic was contagious and the bulk of the North Carolina militia also broke and ran almost immediately. William Gipson, a North Carolina militiaman, would later give a remarkably candid account of this, 'I was among the first that fled,' he stated. 'The cause of that I cannot tell, except that everyone I saw was about to do the same. It was instantaneous. There was no effort to rally, no encouragement to fight. Officers and men joined in the flight.' Stevens himself, writing to the Governor of Virginia, Thomas Jefferson, made no effort to disguise the ugly truth. 'Picture it as bad as you possibly can,' he wrote, 'and it will not be as bad as it really is.' One North Carolina unit, stationed adjacent to the veterans of the 2nd Maryland Brigade, held firm for a while. The Caswell County Militia of Lieutenant-Colonel Henry Dixon stood its ground even when its commanding officer was taken to the rear having been wounded in the neck.

When Cornwallis found de Kalb on the Camden battlefield, he allegedly said, 'I am sorry, sir, to see you. Not sorry that you are vanquished, but sorry to see you so badly wounded.' De Kalb died three days later. (Print Collection, Miriam and Ira D. Wallach Division of Arts, Prints and Photographs, The New York Public Library)

The battle, probably less than 15 minutes old at this point, was now splitting into two separate areas. The Maryland reserve brigade had shown tremendous steadfastness as the fleeing militia swept through their ranks. Calmly letting the panic-stricken men through, the Marylanders had then re-formed and started forward again. Gates was not to prove so resilient. Swept away on the tide of fleeing militia, his army was now without its general and his reputation was never to recover. With the 1st Maryland Brigade occupied by the British 23rd Regiment and light infantry, the bulk of the British army was able to concentrate on the men of the 2nd Maryland Brigade and the lone North Carolina regiment. The battlefield was by now shrouded in gun smoke, and with no breeze to clear the air the sequence of events became less clear. It is evident, however, that the American right wing was more than holding its own. In a punishing fight with Rawdon's Volunteers of Ireland, the Maryland and Delaware troops advanced and, according to some reports, captured Rawdon himself for a brief period. Rawdon reported that the Americans targeted the Volunteers of Ireland standards, triggering a furious response from the provincials. De Kalb led a bayonet charge that threatened to break the British left and there may even have been a victory cheer from the exultant Americans. The 1st Maryland Brigade, however, was slowly being pushed away from the right wing, bending back under the pressure until it was at a sharp angle to the right wing. The gap between the two American formations, estimated to be around 200 yards, proved decisive. The 33rd Regiment, although it had already suffered terribly, was now able to turn on the exposed flank of the American right. Williams, flying around the battlefield, found the 2nd Maryland Brigade about to break and exhorted

At some point during the battle of Camden, a Delaware officer lost this button from his coat, which was found on the battlefield more than 200 years later. Whether the officer lost anything more serious is, of course, not known. (Photograph by Don Troiani)

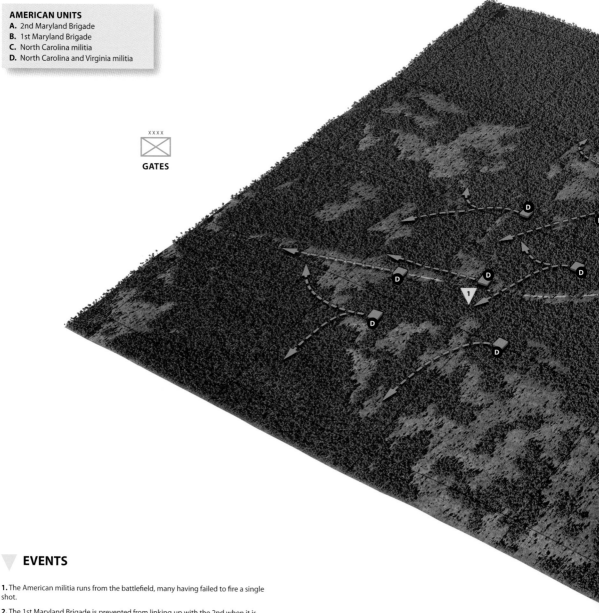

AMERICAN UNITS
A. 2nd Maryland Brigade
B. 1st Maryland Brigade
C. North Carolina militia
D. North Carolina and Virginia militia

GATES

EVENTS

1. The American militia runs from the battlefield, many having failed to fire a single shot.

2. The 1st Maryland Brigade is prevented from linking up with the 2nd when it is engaged by the 23rd Regiment and the British light infantry.

3. Steadied by the presence of the veteran Maryland and Delaware troops in the 2nd Maryland Brigade, a group of North Carolina militia (including several former Continentals) stands firm.

4. The 2nd Brigade has advanced and withdrawn several times, threatening at one point to break the Volunteers of Ireland, but is now also attacked by the 33rd Regiment.

5. The 71st Regiment is ordered forward to reinforce the British assault on the remaining American units.

6. The British Legion cavalry ride through the gap between the two American sections, finally forcing the Continentals to retreat.

THE BATTLE OF CAMDEN: SECOND PHASE

16 August 1780. With most of the American militia fleeing the battlefield, British units close in on the two remaining Maryland brigades.

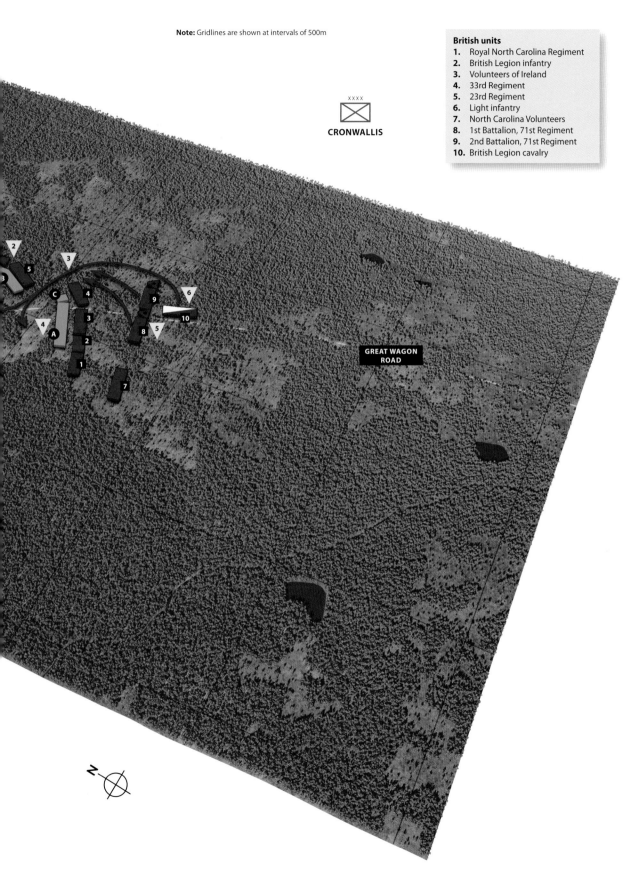

Note: Gridlines are shown at intervals of 500m

xxxx

CRONWALLIS

British units
1. Royal North Carolina Regiment
2. British Legion infantry
3. Volunteers of Ireland
4. 33rd Regiment
5. 23rd Regiment
6. Light infantry
7. North Carolina Volunteers
8. 1st Battalion, 71st Regiment
9. 2nd Battalion, 71st Regiment
10. British Legion cavalry

GREAT WAGON
ROAD

the men of his own regiment, the 6th, to stand. The reply of Lieutenant-Colonel Benjamin Ford, as recorded by Williams, was poignant: 'They have done all that can be asked of them.'

The gap between the two remaining bodies of American troops was just the sort of opportunity Tarleton had been waiting for. Cornwallis ordered the Legion cavalry forward and they poured through the gap before fanning left and right to attack both American positions from the rear. The reserves of the 71st Regiment also entered the fray at this point, plugging the gap between the two British groups. Almost incredibly, it appears that the hard-pressed Continentals did not break and run, but rather were split into smaller parties that surrendered, fought on or retreated. Many escaped through the swamps on the flank of the battlefield and it appears that one of the last men to fall was de Kalb, who was riddled with bullet and bayonet wounds when Cornwallis found him, either slumped against a tree or a wagon depending on whose account you believe. De Kalb was to die three days later.

The battle had lasted just three-quarters of an hour, and had been far from one-sided, but the result was indisputable. Gates' grand army had given the British a hard fight, but it simply no longer existed. 'In short,' an anonymous officer of the Volunteers of Ireland commented, 'it is an army annihilated.'

THE AFTERMATH

The immediate aftermath of the battle of Camden saw Gates ride 180 miles to Hillsborough in three days. This remarkable flight destroyed the reputation of one of America's most distinguished generals and is difficult to explain. Gates himself claimed that he was unable to resist the tide of fleeing militia and was simply carried from the battlefield. Then, according to the man himself, he needed to find a suitable place to rebuild the army. Although many understood his initial removal from the scene (and his attempts to rally the militia are an accepted aspect of the

A monument to de Kalb, placed at the spot on the battlefield where he is believed to have fallen, mortally wounded, on 16 August 1780. (Photo by Stuart Morgan)

battle), few could believe that he really needed to continue for 180 miles. Nathanael Greene would later weigh in with a personal opinion on the battle of Camden, reassuring Gates that he had been unlucky but that his battle leadership had not been wanting. Alexander Hamilton was not so generous, writing acidly that Gates' ride to Hillsborough 'does admirable credit to the activity of a man at his time of life. But it disgraces the general.'

The precipitate flight from the battlefield has influenced historians' opinions of Gates and many have chosen to interpret him as an incompetent general who was 'found out' at Camden. If he was actually marching to battle on the night of 15–16 August those charges may be justified. If, as seems likely, he had the far more modest aim of assuming a strong position to threaten the British post at Camden, then he was extremely unlucky to bump into the British army en route. In the northern theatre, in the early campaigns of the war, Washington had been able to keep his army intact largely because, in General Howe, he faced an opponent who was incapable of quick decisions and quick movements. Gates' greatest misfortune was that he was facing a general of a very different sort.

THE STAND OF THE CONTINENTALS AT CAMDEN (PP. 82–83)

Although only lasting around three quarters of an hour, the battle of Camden was marked by exceptionally fierce fighting during its second phase. Following the collapse of the militia that comprised the left wing of the American army, British forces were able to concentrate on the right wing, the Continental soldiers of the 1st and 2nd Maryland Brigades.

The 33rd Regiment had suffered badly while deploying from column to line at the opening of the battle, but had retained cohesion and was able to swing against the flank of the 2nd Maryland Brigade, comprising Maryland and Delaware troops.

To the left of the picture, the Volunteers of Ireland (1) can be seen also engaging the American line. Lord Rawdon was so delighted with the performance of his regiment at the battle that he ordered a silver medal cast and awarded it to several of his men.

The 1st Maryland Brigade (2), which had tried to advance to form part of the main American line, can be seen in the background on the right of the scene, being engaged by the 23rd

Regiment. This prevented them from linking up with the 2nd Maryland Brigade.

De Kalb, who commanded the American troops in this area (3), was reportedly amazed when told that Gates had fled and that the battle was lost. Stress and confusion, as well as the lack of any sort of breeze (which meant that gunpowder smoke hung heavily in the air by the end of the engagement), can perhaps excuse de Kalb for not realising that the entire left wing of Gates' army had disintegrated.

Fighting alongside the Marylanders in the centre of the scene is a group of North Carolina militia (4). Although most of their comrades had fled, one regiment (which included former Continental officers in its ranks) managed to hold its ground, steadied by the presence of the Maryland and Delaware troops. It is uncertain how long they stood, but bayonet wounds suffered by several of the militia suggest at least some of them held out to the bitter end.

The Virginia Continentals had been lost at Charlestown and now the Maryland and Delaware line had been shattered at Camden. Otho Williams attempted to put numbers on the devastation, listing losses in the Maryland regiments as three lieutenant-colonels, two majors, 15 captains, 13 subalterns, two staff officers, 52 NCOs, 34 musicians and 711 rank and file. Of the Delaware Regiment, an estimated ten officers and 60 privates were taken prisoner, with around 70 killed and the same number wounded (some of the wounded were also captured, although Francis Marion would subsequently free around half of the captives). The Marylanders were not finished, but the severity of their mauling is demonstrated by the fact that the 2nd Brigade was subsequently reorganized as a single regiment, with the Delawares now providing just two companies. The Americans had also lost a brave commander in de Kalb and would soon lose Smallwood of the Marylanders. Disgusted at not being chosen to take command of the remains of the army, he left active service.

Nathanael Greene offered support to Gates after the carnage at Camden, reassuring the vanquished general that his conduct on the battle had not been the unmitigated disaster many others were claiming. (Anne S. K. Brown Military Collection)

Command instead went to Nathanael Greene, who took over from Gates on 3 December.

It did not take long for American resilience to reassert itself. Colonel Josias Hall, of the 4th Maryland Regiment, reckoned morale was already recovering by 28 August. Hall, veteran of four 'general defeats' as he termed them, was the personal manifestation of the spirit later invoked by Greene when he said of the American soldiers: 'We fight, get beat, rise, and fight again.'

British losses in the battle of Camden were detailed more fully, with the 33rd Regiment and Volunteers of Ireland suffering most, with 100 and 87 total casualties respectively. The total number of men killed, wounded and missing, 324, does not seem excessive for a victory of such magnitude, but it continued the process of weakening the British army that had been ongoing since Lexington and Concord. Although usually left in command of the battlefield, the British were conforming to a dire prediction made back in 1775, when Adjutant General Harvey foresaw that they would be 'destroyed by damned driblets'.

The aftermath

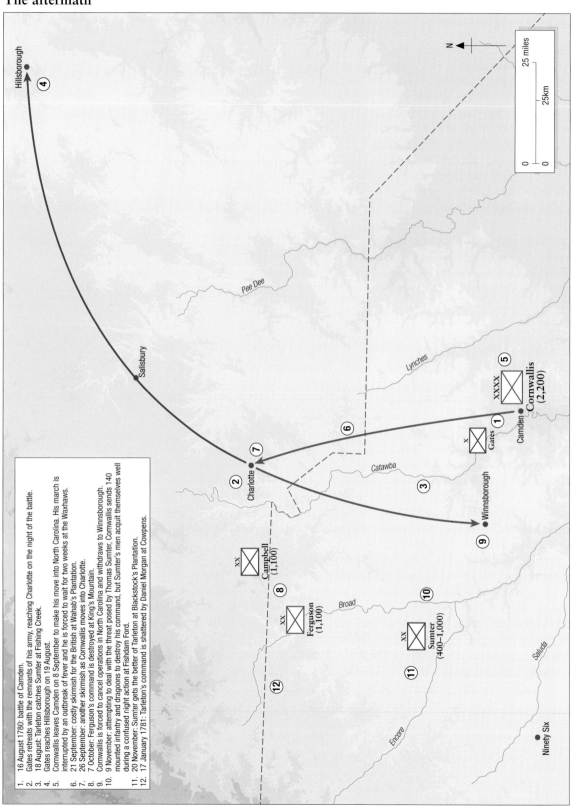

1. 16 August 1780: battle of Camden.
2. Gates retreats with the remnants of his army, reaching Charlotte on the night of the battle.
3. 18 August: Tarleton catches Sumter at Fishing Creek.
4. Gates reaches Hillsborough on 19 August.
5. Cornwallis leaves Camden on 8 September to make his move into North Carolina. His march is interrupted by an outbreak of fever and he is forced to wait for two weeks at the Waxhaws.
6. 21 September: costly skirmish for the British at Wahab's Plantation.
7. 26 September: another skirmish as Cornwallis moves into Charlotte.
8. 7 October: Ferguson's command is destroyed at King's Mountain.
9. Cornwallis is forced to cancel operations in North Carolina and withdraws to Winnsborough.
10. 9 November: attempting to deal with the threat posed by Thomas Sumter, Cornwallis sends 140 mounted infantry and dragoons to destroy his command, but Sumter's men acquit themselves well during a confused night action at Fishdam Ford.
11. 20 November: Sumter gets the better of Tarleton at Blackstock's Plantation.
12. 17 January 1781: Tarleton's command is shattered by Daniel Morgan at Cowpens.

86

In the immediate aftermath of Camden, however, it was the Americans who appeared to be facing that fate. Tarleton was unleashed once more on the morning of 17 August and began to stalk Sumter's command along the Wateree River. The following day, with his Legion infantry exhausted and unable to continue, Tarleton 'doubled up' 60 of them on the mounts of 100 dragoons and pushed on before finding Sumter's men, apparently oblivious of their situation, at Fishing Creek. Tarleton, as always, launched an attack immediately and destroyed Sumter's command. Casualties were again high – 150 Americans killed, with 300 captured for the loss of just 16 killed and wounded on the British side. Tarleton also recaptured 100 British prisoners and more than 40 wagonloads of supplies.

The British once more appeared to be in control of South Carolina, but Cornwallis had already decided that the long-term tranquillity of the colony could be secured only by a move into North Carolina. This conviction would ultimately lead him into Virginia and finally to Yorktown. For now, he prepared to move into North Carolina supported by 1,000 militia under Ferguson. Things started to go wrong on 7 October. On the same day that Ferguson and 400 of his men were dying at King's Mountain under a merciless assault from the fierce 'overmountain men', Nathanael Greene was appointed to take over from Gates. Greene detached Brigadier-General Daniel Morgan to keep Cornwallis occupied while he reorganized the main American army and Cornwallis countered by sending 1,100 men under Tarleton, no doubt expecting to hear a familiar story of pursuit, capture and destruction. Cornwallis did indeed hear such a story, but the destruction was Tarleton's, as Morgan displayed a masterful tactical touch at the battle of Cowpens on 17 January 1781.

Both King's Mountain and Cowpens showed what American militia could do if utilized properly. Gates had asked them to stand in line and face British

The Change of Command. Greene officially took over from Gates on 3 December 1780, in front of the Mecklenburg Court House in Charlotte, North Carolina. (Painting by Werner Willis)

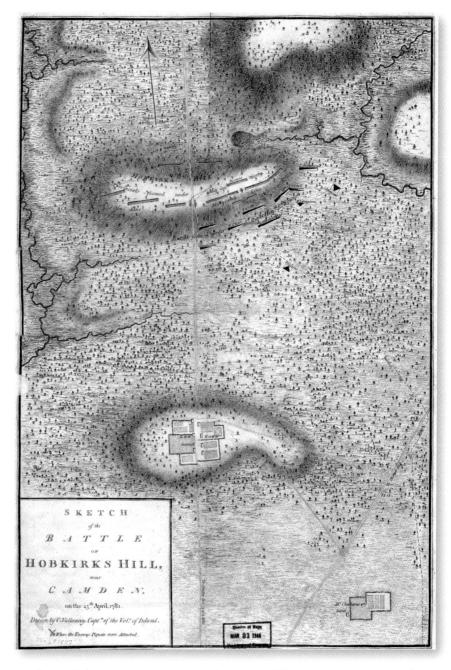

regulars, while at King's Mountain they were able to swarm around a force of enemy militia and whittle them down to nothing. At Cowpens, Morgan demonstrated that militia could play a role in a pitched battle, but only as a sort of 'crumple zone', an advanced line to break up an enemy's advance. Morgan did not ask his militia to stand toe to toe with Tarleton's men, but allowed them to fall back in an organized manner behind his more experienced troops. Simply by knowing they were expected to retire, the militia were able to hold their nerve and even rejoin the battle later.

Cornwallis had lost men he could not replace and, importantly, the spell Tarleton had cast over the south had been broken. Still determined to press

on, Cornwallis made the fateful decision to pursue Greene's steadily retreating Americans, a decision immortalized in one of the most evocative passages written about the war, by Brigadier-General Charles O'Hara. '… without baggage, necessaries, or provisions of any sort for officer or soldier,' O'Hara wrote, 'in the most barren inhospitable, unhealthy part of North America, opposed to the most savage, inveterate, perfidious, cruel enemy, with zeal and with bayonets only, it was resolved to follow Greene's army to the end of the world.'

Guilford Courthouse was not exactly the end of the world, but on 15 March 1781, Cornwallis was forced to buy a victory at the cost of a quarter of his army. The price was too steep and Greene, able to get beat, rise and fight again, kept the core of his army together. With Cornwallis moving into

Virginia, Greene took his men to South Carolina and set about undoing the work of the previous campaign. This included the Second Battle of Camden, Hobkirk's Hill, which may have been another defeat for Greene but was also another sapping of British strength, leading to Rawdon abandoning the post. Ninety Six was besieged, relieved and then abandoned as the British position steadily contracted. Eutaw Springs followed a by-now familiar pattern as the British could claim a tactical victory, only to be forced to fall back once more. Eventually, all they had left was Charleston. The British were back where they had started and their strategy, of pacifying the south with the support of loyalist units, was in tatters.

THE BATTLEFIELD TODAY

Although Charleston is now a major city there are still little corners where a glimpse of its revolutionary past can be found. The Charleston Museum, in fact, is the oldest museum in America and was founded before the revolution, in 1773. The Pringle mansion, used as headquarters for the British during the war, is still standing (the house was also used by Union troops during the American Civil War). You can visit St Michael's Church, which was used as a lookout post by the Americans during the siege. Fort Moultrie, which saw action in both wars, has been restored and visitors can now get a taste for both its Revolutionary War and Civil War past.

The battlefield of Camden has been the subject of a determined and remarkable preservation effort. Longleaf pine was recently replanted in an attempt to restore the battlefield to its 1780 condition and there are many markers and notice boards to guide a visitor through the battle. An extensive archaeological survey in 2009 helped to identify more accurately the exact site of the battle, analysing the concentration of musket balls and case shot in order to determine where the most intense fighting took place. The original road along which the two armies marched on the fateful night of 15–16 August can still be seen as a slight depression to the west of the modern road that now runs through the battlefield, and a marker has been placed on the spot where de Kalb is believed to have fallen.

Camden itself has much to intrigue the historian, with period buildings, the remains of military structures and a revolutionary war museum. Guided tours are available to allow you to 'spend a few peaceful hours where the

Markers and information boards are in abundance at the site of the battle of Camden, making it one of the best preserved battlefields of the entire war. (Photo by Stuart Morgan)

The monument to de Kalb in Camden: 'German by birth, but in principle, citizen of the world. His love of liberty induced him to leave the old world to assist the citizens of the new, in their struggle for independence.' (Photo by Stuart Morgan)

The site of Buford's defeat has been preserved and is now festooned with information boards, monuments and markers. (Photo by Stuart Morgan)

British spent a rough year!' The Kershaw mansion, used by Cornwallis as his headquarters even though it was unfinished at the time, has been rebuilt (it was burned down in 1865) and the foundations of the powder magazine constructed in 1777 can still be seen, as well as the remains of the fortifications that surrounded it. A monument to de Kalb can be found in front of Bethesda Presbyterian Church, on the street named after the fallen general.

BUFORD BATTLEGROUND

IN ORDER THAT ALL MAY CONTINUE TO SHARE
THE SENTIMENTS OF THAT GROUP OF
PATRIOTIC CITIZENS OF LANCASTER COUNTY
WHO ERECTED A MONUMENT HERE ON
JUNE 2, 1860
THE INSCRIPTIONS OF THIS MEMORIAL
ARE THE SAME AS THOSE
ON THE ORIGINAL MONUMENT

ERECTED BY
WAXHAWS CHAPTER
DAUGHTERS OF THE AMERICAN REVOLUTION
AND
LANCASTER COUNTY HISTORICAL COMMISSION

MAY 1955

A monument at the site of the battle of Waxhaws was erected in 1860 but is now difficult to read – a newer monument was commissioned by the Waxhaws Chapter of the Daughters of the American Revolution in 1955. The site also includes the mass grave where many of Buford's unfortunate soldiers were laid to rest. The location of 'Buford's Bloody Battleground' is highlighted by a battlefield marker.

In May 1955 a new monument was erected at the site of the battle of Waxhaws, bearing the same inscription as the original. The reverse side refers to 'The cruelty and barbarous massacre committed on this occasion by Tarleton and his command after the surrender of Col. Buford and his regiment'. (Photo by Stuart Morgan)

FURTHER READING

There is a wealth of primary source material available for deeper study of the actions in South Carolina in 1780. Before delving into these, a good grounding can be found in the standard works on the War of Independence and several recent books offer valuable new insights into various aspects. *Fusiliers: How the British Army Lost America but Learned to Fight*, by Mark Urban, provides a fascinating study of the 23rd Regiment in North America, including a compelling reconstruction of the battle of Camden from the perspective of the regiment. *Patriot Battles: How the War of Independence Was Fought*, by Michael Stephenson, also sheds light on the experience of the average fighting man in 18th-century warfare, helping to bring the battles to life and making events far more understandable. Matthew H. Spring's *With Zeal and With Bayonets Only: The British Army on Campaign in North America, 1775–1783* offers equally valuable insights.

Those wishing to get deeper into the events surrounding the siege of Charleston could not do better than Carl P. Borick's *A Gallant Defense: The Siege of Charleston, 1780*, a wonderful book that offers a tremendous level of detail on the siege from both perspectives. The outbreak of skirmishes, ambushes and small-scale battles that characterized the latter part of the campaign dealt with in this book are exhaustively chronicled in *Nothing But Blood and Slaughter: The Revolutionary War in the Carolinas, Volume Two*, a real labour of love from Patrick O'Kelley. British generals from the war tend to be neglected by historians and you have to go back to 1970 for a full-length study of Cornwallis. Franklin and Mary Wickwire's *Cornwallis and the War of Independence* remains a valuable resource. Clinton is not only the subject of William B. Willcox's superb *Portrait of a General: Sir Henry Clinton in the War of Independence*, his own narrative explaining his conduct in the war is also available in *The American Rebellion: The British Commander-in-Chief's Narrative of his Campaigns, 1775–1782*, edited by Willcox.

Horatio Gates' fascinating story is told well in *The Generals of Saratoga* by Max M. Mintz and he is also given a chapter in *George Washington's Generals and Opponents: Their Exploits and Leadership*, by George Athan Billias. Benjamin Lincoln is also covered in this book (as are Clinton and Cornwallis).

A great starting place for deeper study of the battle itself is *The Battle of Camden: A Documentary History*, by Jim Piecuch. This valuable book draws together primary source documents from officers and soldiers on both sides of the Camden campaign, enabling the enthusiast to hear the story straight from the mouths of the men who fought the battle. Of equal value, although it sticks mostly to the British side of the story, are the volumes of *The Cornwallis Papers: The Campaigns of 1780 and 1781 in the Southern Theatre of the American Revolutionary War*, as edited by Ian Saberton. Volumes I and II are of most relevance to this book. Anyone interested in the mercurial British cavalry commander Banastre Tarleton can read his own account of the campaign in *A History of the Campaigns of 1780 and 1781 in the Southern Provinces of North America*.

INDEX